WEEKENDS

ARE

ENTERTAINING

from Cocktail Parties and Brunches to Dinner for Two or Twenty

◆ ◆ ◆

TIME
LIFE®
BOOKS

TIME-LIFE BOOKS, ALEXANDRIA, VIRGINIA

TIME-LIFE BOOKS IS A DIVISION OF TIME LIFE INC.

TIME-LIFE CUSTOM PUBLISHING

VICE PRESIDENT and PUBLISHER	Terry Newell
Project Manager	Jennifer Pearce
Director of Sales	Neil Levin
Director of New Product Development	Regina Hall
Managing Editor	Donia Ann Steele
Production Manager	Carolyn Mills Bounds
Quality Assurance Manager	Miriam P. Newton

Produced by Rebus, Inc.
New York, New York

Illustrations
William Neeper

Second printing.
Printed in U.S.A.

Library of Congress Cataloging-in-Publication Data
Weekends are entertaining: from cocktail parties and brunches to
dinner for two or twenty/ from the editors of Time-Life Books.
        p. cm. -- (Everyday cookbooks)
Includes index.
ISBN 0-7835-4833-8
1. Entertaining. I. Time-Life Books. II. Series.
TX731.W44   1996
642'.4--dc20   96-12345
                                                                    CIP

Introduction

Weekends Are Entertaining! They can bring boisterous laughter by the pool or a relaxing afternoon in a hammock. But best of all, weekends mean enjoying great food with family and friends, on a leisurely schedule that makes cooking much more fun. Planning a romantic dessert for two? An entire meal for twenty? Here are more than 100 recipes offering great variety, from favorites like Strawberry Shortcake to new exciting twists such as French Toast Waffles or international delights like Egg Rolls. Look for appetizers and snacks like Spicy Buffalo Chicken Wings, main course dishes such as Ham and Seafood Jambalaya, side dishes like Sweet Potato Biscuits—even desserts such as Red, White, and Blue Pie. Serve Glazed Peach Coffeecake for brunch, or Banana Daiquiris after a softball game!

This cookbook makes planning a party easier with these highlights:

- You'll find recipes for all the ways you like to entertain, whether dressy or casual, indoors or out. Make Nachos in a jiffy or impress your guests with a Raspberry Soufflé. Warm up with Hot Spiced Cider or cool off with Orange Lemonade.

- The "Menu Suggestions" section helps you mix and match recipes for anything from a Picnic in the Park to a Hearty Sunday Brunch or a Holiday Feast.

- Some of the recipes—labeled "Extra-Quick"—take under 30 minutes to prepare. They are marked with this symbol: ⏱. (A full listing of these recipes is included in the index under "Extra-Quick.")

- To help you accommodate health-conscious guests, we've included some recipes that get fewer than 30 percent of their calories from fat. These recipes are labeled "Low-Fat" and are marked with this symbol: ♡. (A full listing of these recipes is included in the index under the heading "Low-Fat.")

Whether you're hosting a child's birthday party or a black-tie cocktail bash, *Weekends Are Entertaining* will be the first guest you invite!

—*Mara Reid Rogers,*
author of numerous cookbooks and
spokesperson for The Everyday Cookbooks™

Contents

DESSERTS

BEVERAGES

MENU SUGGESTIONS

INDEX

APPETIZERS AND SNACKS

STUFFED MUSHROOM CAPS

MAKES 18

1 CUP RICOTTA CHEESE
¼ CUP FINELY CHOPPED PARSLEY
¼ POUND PROSCIUTTO (THINLY SLICED ITALIAN CURED HAM), FINELY CHOPPED
2 TEASPOONS SALT
PINCH OF BLACK PEPPER
1 TABLESPOON FRESH LEMON JUICE
4 TABLESPOONS OLIVE OIL
18 MEDIUM MUSHROOM CAPS
2½ OUNCES MOZZARELLA CHEESE, CUT INTO ¼-INCH PIECES

1. Preheat the oven to 400°.

2. In a large bowl, combine the ricotta cheese, parsley, prosciutto, salt, pepper, and lemon juice. Beat vigorously until the ingredients are well combined and the mixture is smooth; set aside.

3. In a medium skillet, warm the oil over medium heat. Drop in the mushroom caps and sauté for about 2 minutes, then turn them over and cook for another minute, or until they are lightly browned.

4. Fill the mushroom caps with the ricotta mixture and top each cap with bits of mozzarella. Arrange the caps side by side in a shallow baking dish or jelly-roll pan and bake for 8 minutes, or until the filling begins to bubble. Slide the caps under a hot broiler for 30 seconds to brown the mozzarella topping. Serve at once.

CHEESE PUFFS

MAKES 2 DOZEN

1 CUP GRATED MONTEREY JACK
   CHEESE
1 CUP GRATED CHEDDAR CHEESE
2 TABLESPOONS FLOUR
1 CUP FRESH CRACKER CRUMBS

3 EGG WHITES
1½ TEASPOONS YELLOW MUSTARD
VEGETABLE OIL FOR DEEP FRYING
SALT

1. In a large bowl, combine the cheeses and the flour. Spread the cracker crumbs on a piece of wax paper and set aside.

2. In another large bowl, beat the egg whites until stiff peaks form. Scoop the egg whites over the cheese mixture with a rubber spatula, add the mustard, and fold the ingredients together gently but thoroughly.

3. To make each cheese puff, spoon a heaping tablespoonful of the cheese mixture and mold it into a ball by placing a second tablespoon on top. Slide the cheese ball off the spoon onto the cracker crumbs and roll it about to coat it evenly. Transfer the cheese ball to a piece of wax paper and set it aside while you proceed to shape and coat the remaining cheese mixture.

4. Pour vegetable oil into a deep fryer or large saucepan to a depth of about 3 inches and warm the oil over medium-high heat until it is very hot.

5. Deep-fry the cheese balls, 4 or 5 at a time, turning them, for about 3 minutes or until they are crisp and golden brown. As they color, transfer them to paper towels to drain.

6. Arrange the cheese puffs attractively on a heated platter, season them lightly with a sprinkling of salt, and serve them while they are still warm.

Spicy Buffalo Chicken Wings

SERVES 6 TO 8

2½ POUNDS CHICKEN WINGS

4 TABLESPOONS UNSALTED BUTTER, MELTED

¼ CUP BARBECUE SAUCE

¼ CUP HOT PEPPER SAUCE

⅛ TEASPOON CAYENNE PEPPER, OR TO TASTE

1 CUP BLUE CHEESE DRESSING

2 CELERY RIBS, CUT INTO STICKS

1. Preheat the oven to 325°. Spray a baking sheet with nonstick cooking spray.

2. Remove the tips from the chicken wings, splitting at the joint. Place the chicken wings on the prepared baking sheet and bake for 30 minutes.

3. Meanwhile, in a small bowl, combine the butter, barbecue sauce, hot pepper sauce, and cayenne pepper.

4. Remove the wings from the oven and place them in a shallow dish. Pour 1 cup of the hot sauce mixture over them; marinate at room temperature for 1 hour.

5. Preheat the broiler.

6. Return the wings to the baking sheet and broil for 15 minutes, or until cooked through, turning and brushing with the remaining marinade every 5 minutes.

7. Pour the blue cheese dressing into a small bowl and place it in the center of a serving platter. Arrange the chicken wings and celery around the bowl and serve.

Potato Skins with Sour Cream and Chives

MAKES 32

8 LARGE BAKING POTATOES
¼ CUP OLIVE OIL
1 TEASPOON CHILI POWDER
1¼ TEASPOONS SALT

1 CUP SOUR CREAM
2 TABLESPOONS CHOPPED FRESH
   CHIVES OR SCALLION GREENS

1. Preheat the oven to 450°. Pierce each potato 2 or 3 times. Place the potatoes on a baking sheet and bake for 50 to 60 minutes, or until tender when pierced with a fork. Set the potatoes aside to cool for 5 minutes.

2. In a small bowl, combine the oil, chili powder, and salt. Cut each potato lengthwise into quarters. Scoop out the potato flesh, leaving a scant ¼-inch shell. Place the potato skins on 2 large baking sheets. Brush with the oil mixture and bake for 15 minutes, or until the potatoes are browned and crisp.

3. Meanwhile, in a small bowl, combine the sour cream and chives and stir until well blended.

4. Serve the potato skins on a large platter with the sour cream and chives on the side for dipping.

Mini Crab Cakes

1 POUND LUMP CRABMEAT, PICKED OVER TO REMOVE ANY BITS OF SHELL OR CARTILAGE

1 CUP CHOPPED SCALLIONS

1 SLICE FIRM-TEXTURED WHITE BREAD, TORN INTO LARGE CRUMBS

¼ CUP CHOPPED PARSLEY

2 EGGS, LIGHTLY BEATEN

2 TABLESPOONS MAYONNAISE

1 TABLESPOON DIJON MUSTARD

2 TEASPOONS WORCESTERSHIRE SAUCE

¼ TEASPOON BLACK PEPPER

1 CUP FINE UNSEASONED DRY BREAD CRUMBS

4 TABLESPOONS BUTTER

HOT PEPPER SAUCE

1. In a large bowl, combine the crabmeat, scallions, large bread crumbs, parsley, eggs, mayonnaise, mustard, Worcestershire sauce, and pepper. Shape the mixture into 24 cakes. Roll each cake in the dry bread crumbs.

2. In a large skillet, melt the butter over medium-high heat until just beginning to smoke. Carefully add the crab cakes, in batches, and cook until browned on one side, 2 to 3 minutes. Gently turn the cakes and cook until browned on the second side, about 2 to 3 minutes. Add more butter if necessary to prevent sticking.

3. Serve the crab cakes hot, with hot pepper sauce on the side.

VERMONT CHEDDAR SPREAD

SERVES 8 TO 10

EXTRA-QUICK

ONE 3-OUNCE PACKAGE CREAM
 CHEESE, AT ROOM TEMPERATURE
4 TABLESPOONS BUTTER, AT ROOM
 TEMPERATURE
½ POUND SHARP WHITE CHEDDAR
 CHEESE, GRATED

3 TABLESPOONS CHOPPED FRESH
 CHIVES
½ TEASPOON DRY MUSTARD
PINCH OF CAYENNE PEPPER
ASSORTED CRACKERS

1. In a medium bowl with an electric mixer, beat the cream cheese and butter until well blended. Beat in the Cheddar cheese until combined. Add the chives, mustard, and cayenne pepper, and beat until fluffy.

2. Transfer the mixture to a crock or bowl. Place the bowl in the center of a serving plate and surround it with the crackers.

KITCHEN NOTE: *Any leftover Cheddar spread makes a delicious sandwich filling: Spread 1 slice of dense whole-grain bread with the Cheddar mixture, and spread the other with mango chutney.*

CORN THINS

MAKES 8 DOZEN

♡ LOW-FAT

1 CUP WHITE CORNMEAL
½ CUP FLOUR
1 TABLESPOON SUGAR
½ TEASPOON SALT
¼ TEASPOON BAKING SODA

¼ TEASPOON BLACK PEPPER, OR MORE
  TO TASTE
½ CUP PLAIN LOW-FAT YOGURT
1 TABLESPOON BUTTER, MELTED

1. Preheat the oven to 350°.

2. In a medium bowl, combine the cornmeal, flour, sugar, salt, baking soda, and pepper. Add the yogurt and butter and stir until well combined.

3. Divide the dough into 2 equal portions. Spray a nonstick baking sheet with nonstick cooking spray; lightly dust a rolling pin with cornmeal. Place one portion of dough on the baking sheet and roll it out to a ¼-inch thickness. Place a sheet of wax paper over the dough and roll it out to a 10-inch square. Remove the wax paper. Using a ruler and a

sharp knife, cut the dough into 2-inch squares, then into triangles; do not separate them.

4. Bake the corn thins 20 minutes, or until crisp and golden. Check after 8 minutes; if they are browning unevenly, turn the baking sheet. Transfer the corn thins to a rack to cool (they will separate as you remove them from the pan).

5. Rinse and respray the baking sheet, then make a second batch of corn thins in the same fashion.

Oven-Baked Potato Chips

SERVES 8

♡ LOW-FAT

8 LARGE IDAHO POTATOES (ABOUT 6
   POUNDS)

PAPRIKA

1. Preheat the oven to 400°.

2. Scrub the potatoes well and cut them crosswise into ⅛-inch-thick slices.

3. Lightly coat a large baking sheet with non-stick cooking spray. Arrange the potato slices in 1 layer, then spray the slices lightly with cooking spray. Sprinkle lightly with paprika.

4. Bake the chips 30 minutes, turning once, then reduce the heat to 300°. Bake another 15 to 20 minutes, or until the chips are crisp and browned. Repeat with the remaining potato slices.

KITCHEN NOTE: *These chips are meant to be eaten while they're fresh and hot; they won't stay crisp if they're stored. For a spicy change, sprinkle the potatoes with chili powder instead of paprika.*

SAUSAGE ROLL

SERVES 8

1½ POUNDS UNCOOKED PLAIN OR
GARLIC PORK SAUSAGE (ABOUT
12 INCHES LONG)
1½ CUPS FLOUR
¼ TEASPOON SALT
6 TABLESPOONS BUTTER, AT ROOM
TEMPERATURE

2 TABLESPOONS VEGETABLE
SHORTENING
3 TO 5 TABLESPOONS ICE WATER
1 EGG BEATEN WITH 1 TEASPOON
WATER
DIJON MUSTARD, FOR DIPPING

1. Prick the sausage in 5 or 6 places and lay it flat in a large skillet; add enough cold water to cover it completely. Bring to a boil over medium heat and simmer, uncovered, for 45 minutes. Transfer the sausage to paper towels to drain and cool. Then split the skin with a sharp knife and peel it off.

2. Meanwhile, in a medium bowl, combine the flour and salt. Cut the butter and shortening into the flour until the mixture is coarse crumbs. Pour 3 tablespoons of ice water over the mixture all at once, toss together lightly, and gather the dough into a ball. If the dough seems crumbly, add up to 2 tablespoons more ice water by drops.

3. Preheat the oven to 375°. Grease a large baking sheet.

4. Roll the dough out ¼ inch thick in a rectangular shape large enough to wrap around

the sausage. Center the cooled sausage on the rectangle. Cut triangles of pastry from each corner of the roll and gently, without stretching the dough, lift the long sides of the pastry up over the sausage. Trim the overlap to an even inch. Brush the lower edge of the pastry with the egg-water mixture and press the upper edge down upon it firmly to secure it.

5. Brush the envelope-like flaps at the ends of the roll with egg mixture, then lift the flaps up over the ends of the sausage and tuck the edges in neatly to seal them. Turn the wrapped sausage over and place it, seam-side down, on the prepared baking sheet. Coat the whole roll with the rest of the egg mixture.

6. Bake the roll for 45 to 50 minutes, or until it is golden brown. Transfer the roll to a large platter and cut it into ¾-inch slices. Serve the mustard on the side.

Potato Knishes

MAKES 14

2 TABLESPOONS BUTTER
1 CUP FINELY CHOPPED ONIONS
2 CUPS COOLED MASHED POTATOES
½ CUP FLOUR

1 EGG
½ TEASPOON SALT
¼ TEASPOON BLACK PEPPER

1. Preheat the oven to 375°. Grease a large baking sheet.

2. In a medium skillet, melt the butter over medium heat. Add the onions and cook, stirring frequently, for 5 minutes, or until they are soft and translucent. Remove from the heat; set aside to cool to room temperature.

3. In a large bowl, combine the mashed potatoes, flour, egg, salt, and pepper. Knead the mixture until it is well combined and smooth.

Divide the mixture into 14 balls, each measuring about 2 inches in diameter. Flatten the balls slightly and top each with about 2 teaspoons of the cooked onions. Pull enough of the potato dough up over the onion filling to enclose it.

4. Place the knishes about 1 inch apart on the prepared baking sheet. Bake for 30 to 35 minutes, or until they are golden brown. Serve hot.

KITCHEN NOTE: *This simplified version of a favorite New York City delicatessen food is delicious with brown or Dijon mustard for dipping. Horseradish or chili sauce are other dipping options.*

Egg Rolls

MAKES 16

3 TABLESPOONS VEGETABLE OIL

½ POUND GROUND PORK

1 TABLESPOON CHINESE RICE WINE, OR
   PALE DRY SHERRY

1 TABLESPOON SOY SAUCE

½ TEASPOON SUGAR

½ POUND SHRIMP, DICED

3 MEDIUM MUSHROOMS, SLICED

4 CUPS FINELY CHOPPED CELERY

2½ TEASPOONS SALT

½ POUND MUNG BEAN SPROUTS

1 TABLESPOON CORNSTARCH DISSOLVED
   IN 2 TABLESPOONS COLD WATER

16 EGG-ROLL WRAPPERS

1 EGG, LIGHTLY BEATEN

3 CUPS PEANUT OIL

DUCK SAUCE

1. In a large wok or skillet, heat 1 tablespoon of the vegetable oil over medium heat. Add the pork and cook for 2 minutes, or until it loses its reddish color. Add the wine, soy sauce, sugar, shrimp, and mushrooms, and cook for 1 minute, or until the shrimp turn pink. Transfer the mixture to a bowl; set aside.

2. Add the remaining 2 tablespoons of vegetable oil to the wok, swirl it about in the pan, then add the celery and stir-fry for 5 minutes. Add the salt and bean sprouts and mix thoroughly together. Return the pork and shrimp mixture to the pan, and stir until all the ingredients are well combined. Stirring constantly, bring the liquid to a boil.

3. Add the cornstarch mixture to the wok, stirring until the cooking liquids have thickened slightly. Transfer the contents of the pan to a bowl and cool to room temperature.

4. For each egg roll, shape about ¼ cup of filling into a cylinder about 4 inches long and an inch in diameter, and place it diagonally across the center of a wrapper. Lift the lower triangular flap over the filling and tuck the point under it, leaving the upper point of the wrapper exposed. Bring each of the 2 small end flaps, 1 at a time, up to the top of the enclosed filling and press the points firmly down. Brush the upper and exposed triangle of dough with egg and then roll the wrapper into a neat package.

5. Warm the peanut oil in a large wok or deep fryer until it is very hot. Place 5 or 6 egg rolls in the hot oil and deep-fry them for 3 to 4 minutes, or until they have become golden brown and are crisp. Transfer the egg rolls to paper towels to drain. Serve the egg rolls warm, with duck sauce on the side.

Pork Wontons

MAKES 40

1 POUND GROUND PORK SHOULDER

1 TABLESPOON CHINESE RICE WINE, OR
  PALE DRY SHERRY

1 TABLESPOON SOY SAUCE

2 TEASPOONS SALT

1 TEASPOON SUGAR

1 TABLESPOON CORNSTARCH

1 TEASPOON GRATED FRESH GINGER

⅛ CUP FINELY CHOPPED SCALLIONS

¼ CUP FINELY CHOPPED CANNED
  WATER CHESTNUTS

1 PACKAGE WONTON SKINS

2 CUPS PEANUT OIL

1. In a large bowl, combine the pork, wine, soy sauce, salt, sugar, cornstarch, and ginger, and mix thoroughly. Stir in the scallions and water chestnuts.

2. To make the wontons, place a teaspoonful of filling in the center of a wonton skin. Fold the bottom corner up over the filling, moisten the edges with a little water, and pinch the edges closed to form a triangle. Fold the 2 bottom corners up over the filled section so they overlap, moisten them, and pinch them together to form a little ring. The filling should be well sealed in.

3. Heat the oil in a deep fryer or a large wok until it is very hot. Deep-fry the filled wontons in several batches until golden, about 5 minutes. Drain the wontons on paper towels and serve immediately.

Hummus with Toasted Pita Wedges

SERVES 6 TO 8

⏲ EXTRA-QUICK

2 CUPS CANNED CHICK PEAS, RINSED
    AND DRAINED
¼ CUP CHOPPED PARSLEY
¼ CUP CHOPPED ONION
½ TEASPOON CHOPPED GARLIC
3 TABLESPOONS FRESH LEMON JUICE

2 TABLESPOONS OLIVE OIL
½ TEASPOON SALT
PINCH OF CAYENNE PEPPER
4 WHOLE-WHEAT PITA BREADS, SPLIT
    AND QUARTERED

1. Place the chick peas in a food processor and process for 30 seconds to 1 minute, or until the chick peas are coarsely chopped. Add the parsley, onion, garlic, lemon juice, and oil, and process until smooth.

2. Transfer the hummus to a serving bowl. Stir in the salt and cayenne pepper.

3. Place the pita bread quarters on a large baking sheet and toast under the broiler for 1 minute.

4. Place the bowl of hummus in the center of a serving platter. Arrange the toasted pita wedges around the bowl and serve.

Variation: *In the Middle East, hummus is often blended with tahini, a thick sesame-seed paste. Try adding 2 to 3 tablespoons of tahini to the mixture for a rich, nutlike flavor.*

ΠACHOS

S E R V E S   8

⏱ E X T R A - Q U I C K

EIGHT 6-INCH CORN TORTILLAS
1¼ CUPS CANNED KIDNEY BEANS,
    RINSED AND DRAINED
¼ TEASPOON CHILI POWDER

2 CUPS SALSA, BOTTLED OR
    HOMEMADE *(PAGE 22)*
1 CUP SHREDDED MONTEREY JACK
    CHEESE

1. Preheat the oven to 500°.

2. Immerse the tortillas 1 at a time in water; drain and lay them on baking sheets. Bake the tortillas for 6 to 7 minutes, or just until crisp, turning them after 4 to 5 minutes. If the tortillas begin to curl, lay another baking sheet on top of them. Remove the tortillas from the baking sheet, using a metal spatula to loosen them if necessary, and set aside to cool. Reduce the oven temperature to 350°.

3. Combine the beans and chili powder in a small skillet and cook over medium heat, mashing the beans with a fork, until the mixture is heated through. Stir in some water, a few drops at a time, until the mixture is smooth and spreadable.

4. Cut each tortilla into 6 wedges, then reassemble the wedges into rounds on the baking sheet.

5. Spread the bean mixture equally over the tortillas and top each with ¼ cup of salsa and 2 tablespoons of cheese. Layer on the remaining salsa and cheese. Bake for 4 to 5 minutes, or until the cheese is melted. Serve hot.

FRESH SALSA WITH TOASTED TORTILLAS

MAKES 5 CUPS

3 LARGE TOMATOES, COARSELY CHOPPED

2 SMALL RED ONIONS, FINELY CHOPPED

4 GARLIC CLOVES, MINCED

2 TABLESPOONS SEEDED, FINELY CHOPPED JALAPEÑO PEPPERS

½ CUP CHOPPED CILANTRO

½ CUP RED WINE VINEGAR

2 TABLESPOONS OLIVE OIL

1 TEASPOON SALT

½ TEASPOON BLACK PEPPER

1 PACKAGE SOFT CORN TORTILLAS, CUT INTO QUARTERS

1. Place the chopped tomatoes in a large bowl (if they are very watery, drain the excess liquid). Add the onions, garlic, jalapeños, cilantro, vinegar, oil, salt, and pepper, and mix until well blended. Let the salsa stand for at least 30 minutes before serving.

2. Preheat the oven to 425°.

3. Working in batches, arrange the tortillas on a large baking sheet and bake a few minutes on each side, until the chips begin to crisp and turn brown. Let the chips cool completely before serving with the salsa.

ZESTY GUACAMOLE

MAKES 6 CUPS

EXTRA-QUICK

6 RIPE AVOCADOS, PEELED AND PITTED
¾ CUP FINELY CHOPPED RED ONION
3 GARLIC CLOVES, MINCED
⅓ CUP FRESH LIME JUICE
⅓ CUP SOUR CREAM
⅓ CUP CHOPPED CILANTRO

1 TABLESPOON CHILI POWDER
1½ TEASPOONS SALT
¾ TEASPOON BLACK PEPPER
½ TEASPOON HOT PEPPER SAUCE,
   OR TO TASTE
TORTILLA CHIPS

1. Place the avocados in a large bowl and mash them lightly with a fork, leaving them slightly chunky.

2. Add the onion, garlic, lime juice, sour cream, cilantro, chili powder, salt, pepper, and hot pepper sauce, and mix until well blended.

If not serving immediately, lay a sheet of heavy-duty plastic wrap directly on the surface of the guacamole, cover the bowl, and refrigerate.

3. Serve the guacamole with tortilla chips.

KITCHEN NOTE: *Hass avocados, which have a pebbly-textured black skin and rich, velvety flesh, make a better guacamole than smooth-skinned green Fuerte avocados. A ripe avocado will yield to gentle finger pressure; if the avocado you buy is not ripe, place it in a paper bag and leave at room temperature for a few days. Placing a tomato in the bag will speed the process.*

Chunky Black Bean Dip

MAKES 6 CUPS

⏱ EXTRA-QUICK

½ POUND BACON (8 TO 12 SLICES)
3 CUPS CHOPPED SCALLIONS
12 GARLIC CLOVES, MINCED
¼ CUP CHILI POWDER
1 TABLESPOON CUMIN
6 CUPS CANNED BLACK BEANS, RINSED
   AND DRAINED

¾ CUP OLIVE OIL
6 DROPS HOT PEPPER SAUCE,
   OR TO TASTE
1½ TEASPOONS SALT
¾ TEASPOON BLACK PEPPER
TORTILLA CHIPS

1. In a large skillet, cook the bacon over medium heat until crisp, about 10 minutes. Reserving 3 tablespoons of fat in the skillet, drain the bacon on paper towels; crumble and set aside.

2. Add the scallions and garlic to the skillet and sauté over medium heat until the scallions are softened but not browned, about 5 minutes. Add the chili powder and cumin and cook, stirring, for 1 minute; set aside.

3. Place the beans in a large bowl and mash them lightly with a fork or a potato masher. Add the oil, hot pepper sauce, salt, and pepper, and mix well. Stir in the scallion mixture and the reserved bacon bits. Serve the bean dip with tortilla chips.

Spinach and Cheese Squares

SERVES 10 TO 12

¼ CUP OLIVE OIL

½ CUP FINELY CHOPPED ONIONS

¼ CUP FINELY CHOPPED SCALLIONS

2 POUNDS FRESH SPINACH, FINELY
  CHOPPED

¼ CUP FINELY CHOPPED DILL OR
  2 TABLESPOONS DRIED

¼ CUP FINELY CHOPPED PARSLEY

½ TEASPOON SALT

PINCH OF BLACK PEPPER

⅓ CUP MILK

½ POUND FETA CHEESE, FINELY
  CHOPPED

4 EGGS, LIGHTLY BEATEN

2 STICKS BUTTER, MELTED

SIXTEEN 16 X 12-INCH SHEETS PHYLLO
  PASTRY DOUGH

1. In a large skillet, warm the olive oil over medium heat. Add the onions and scallions and cook for 5 minutes, or until they are soft and translucent. Stir in the spinach, cover tightly, and cook for 5 minutes. Add the dill, parsley, salt, and pepper and, stirring and shaking the pan, cook, uncovered, for about 10 minutes, or until most of the liquid in the skillet has evaporated. Transfer the spinach mixture to a deep bowl and stir in the milk. Cool to room temperature, then add the cheese and slowly beat in the eggs.

2. Preheat the oven to 300°. Coat the bottom and sides of a 12 x 7 x 2-inch baking dish with some of the melted butter. Unfold the phyllo and cover it with a damp kitchen towel (keep the phyllo covered while you work to keep it from drying out). Line the dish with a sheet of phyllo, pressing the edges of the pastry firmly into the corners and against the sides of the dish. Brush the entire surface of the pastry with about 2 to 3 teaspoons of butter, spreading it all the way to the outside edges and lay another sheet of phyllo on top. Spread with another 2 to 3 teaspoons of butter and continue constructing the pie in this fashion until you have used 8 layers of the phyllo in all.

3. Spread the spinach mixture evenly over the last layer of phyllo and smooth it out into the corners. Place another sheet of the phyllo on top, coat with butter, and repeat with the remaining layers of phyllo and butter as before. Trim the excess pastry from around the rim of the dish. Brush the top of the pie with the remaining butter and bake for 1 hour, or until crisp and delicately browned. Cut into small squares and serve.

CHEESE FONDUE

SERVES 8 TO 10

⏱ EXTRA-QUICK

1 GARLIC CLOVE, PEELED
2 CUPS DRY WHITE WINE
1 TEASPOON FRESH LEMON JUICE
1 POUND SHREDDED SWISS CHEESE
3 TABLESPOONS FLOUR

SALT
BLACK PEPPER
1 LARGE LOAF FRENCH BREAD, CUT
   INTO LARGE CUBES

1. Rub the inside of a fondue pot or flame-proof casserole with the garlic. Pour in the wine and lemon juice, and over medium heat, bring it almost to a boil. Mix the cheese with the flour and add the mixture by handful to the pot, stirring constantly in a figure 8 motion. Continue to stir until the cheese melts into a thick cream. Season to taste with salt and pepper. Set the pot over a low flame. Regulate the heat so that the fondue simmers gently but does not boil.

2. Serve the fondue with the cubes of bread. If the fondue becomes too thick as it simmers, thin it with some heated wine stirred in by the tablespoonful.

KITCHEN NOTE: *Perhaps the most delicious and convivial way to enjoy fine Swiss cheese, fondue probably originated in the French-speaking part of the Swiss Alps ("fondu" means "melted" in French). The cheese mixture is kept hot in a special pot over a flame; long-handled forks are used to dip the chunks of bread. Use an aged, imported cheese, which will melt smoothly. Try a well-aged Emmentaler (that's the true Swiss name for what we call "Swiss cheese") or a good Swiss Gruyère.*

Scandinavian-Style Canapés

SERVES 4

🕐 EXTRA-QUICK ♡ LOW-FAT

¼ CUP PLAIN LOW-FAT YOGURT

2 TEASPOONS DIJON MUSTARD

1 TABLESPOON CHOPPED FRESH DILL, PLUS 16 DILL SPRIGS

16 SLICES COCKTAIL PUMPERNICKEL BREAD

SIXTEEN ¼-INCH-THICK CUCUMBER SLICES

1 MEDIUM RED BELL PEPPER, CUT INTO SIXTEEN 1-INCH SQUARES

2 OUNCES SMOKED SALMON, CUT INTO 16 PIECES

1. In a small bowl stir together the yogurt, mustard, and chopped dill.

2. Spread the bread with the yogurt mixture. Place a cucumber slice and a bell pepper square on each piece of bread and top with a piece of salmon and a dill sprig.

3. Arrange the canapés on a platter and serve. If not serving the canapés immediately, cover the platter tightly with plastic wrap and refrigerate.

Vegetarian Pâté

SERVES 16

♡ LOW - FAT

1 CUP KASHA (MEDIUM GRAIN)
1 TEASPOON PLUS 1 TABLESPOON
 PEANUT OIL
2 CUPS THINLY SLICED MUSHROOMS
1 CUP FINELY CHOPPED ONION
1 CUP SHREDDED CARROTS
¼ CUP WHEAT GERM

¼ CUP DIJON MUSTARD
4 LARGE EGG WHITES
1 TEASPOON SALT
½ TEASPOON DRIED ROSEMARY
½ TEASPOON DRIED THYME
¼ TEASPOON BLACK PEPPER

1. Stir the kasha into 2 cups of boiling water, reduce the heat to low, cover, and simmer 8 to 10 minutes, or until the kasha is fluffy and the water is absorbed; set aside, covered.

2. Brush a 9 x 4-inch glass loaf pan with 1 teaspoon of oil; set aside.

3. Heat the remaining oil in a large nonstick skillet over medium heat. Stir in the mushrooms, onion, and carrots, cover and cook about 5 minutes, or until the mushrooms release their liquid. Uncover the skillet, reduce the heat to low and cook, stirring, about 10 minutes, or until the vegetables are soft and all the liquid has evaporated; transfer to a large bowl and set aside.

4. Preheat the oven to 350°.

5. Stir the kasha into the vegetable mixture. Add the wheat germ, 1 tablespoon of the mustard, the egg whites, salt, rosemary, thyme, and pepper and stir until well blended.

6. Transfer the kasha mixture to the prepared pan. Cover the pâté with foil, prick the foil in several places with a fork and place the loaf pan in a large roasting pan. Add ½ inch of hot water to the roasting pan and bake the pâté 1½ hours.

7. When the pâté is done, cool it on a rack for 30 minutes, then refrigerate it overnight. Turn the pâté out onto a platter and use a sharp knife to cut it into 16 slices. Serve the remaining mustard with the pâté.

KITCHEN NOTE: *Kasha is the American market term for roasted buckwheat. You'll find kasha at most supermarkets, alongside the rice or in the Jewish foods section.*

MAIN DISHES

HERBED OVEN-FRIED CHICKEN

SERVES 4

♡ LOW-FAT

1 TABLESPOON VEGETABLE OIL

⅓ CUP CHILI SAUCE

3 TABLESPOONS FRESH LEMON JUICE

3 TABLESPOONS SOY SAUCE

¼ TEASPOON SALT

¼ TEASPOON BLACK PEPPER

1½ TEASPOONS ITALIAN SEASONING

4 BONE-IN CHICKEN BREAST HALVES,
 SKIN REMOVED

½ CUP FLOUR

¼ CUP YELLOW CORNMEAL

¼ CUP CHOPPED PARSLEY

1. In a large bowl, combine the oil, chili sauce, lemon juice, soy sauce, salt, pepper, and Italian seasoning. Add the chicken breast halves and coat evenly. Cover and refrigerate 3 to 5 hours, turning often.

2. Preheat the oven to 350°. Spray a large baking sheet with nonstick cooking spray.

3. Combine the flour, cornmeal, and parsley on a plate. Dredge the chicken breast halves in the flour mixture, coating evenly. Place the chicken, breast-side up, on the prepared baking sheet. Bake the chicken for 1 hour, or until the juices run clear.

KITCHEN NOTE: *For quicker cleanup, combine the marinade ingredients in a large, heavy-duty zip-seal bag; add the chicken, seal the bag, and shake to coat the chicken with the marinade.*

BARBECUED SPARERIBS WITH ORANGE SAUCE

SERVES 6 TO 8

2 CUPS KETCHUP

1 CUP ORANGE MARMALADE

2 TABLESPOONS TOMATO PASTE

2 TABLESPOONS DIJON MUSTARD

2 TABLESPOONS WORCESTERSHIRE
  SAUCE

1 MEDIUM ONION, MINCED

2 GARLIC CLOVES, MINCED

2 SLABS LEAN SPARERIBS (ABOUT
  3½ POUNDS TOTAL)

1. In a medium saucepan, bring the ketchup, orange marmalade, tomato paste, mustard, Worcestershire sauce, onion, and garlic to a boil over medium-high heat. Reduce the heat to medium-low and simmer, partially covered, for 30 minutes, stirring occasionally.

2. Preheat the oven to 375°. Line a baking sheet with foil.

3. Place the spareribs, meaty-side up, on the prepared baking sheet. Brush the spareribs with one-third of the barbecue sauce and bake for 20 minutes.

4. Turn the spareribs over, coat with half of the remaining barbecue sauce, and bake for another 20 minutes.

5. Turn the spareribs meaty-side up again, coat with the remaining barbecue sauce, and bake for 20 minutes.

6. Cut the spareribs into serving pieces and serve hot or cold.

Cajun-Style Chicken

SERVES 8 TO 10

1 CUP FLOUR

3 LARGE GARLIC CLOVES, MINCED

½ TEASPOON PEPPER, PREFERABLY
 WHITE

¼ TEASPOON CAYENNE PEPPER

1½ TEASPOONS THYME

1½ TEASPOONS SALT

2½ POUNDS CHICKEN PARTS

ABOUT 4 CUPS PEANUT OIL, FOR
 FRYING

2 MEDIUM ONIONS, CHOPPED

2 MEDIUM RED BELL PEPPERS, CHOPPED

2 CELERY RIBS, CHOPPED

1 CUP CHOPPED LEEKS, OR 1 CUP
 CHOPPED ONION

ONE 14-OUNCE CAN WHOLE TOMATOES

ONE 15-OUNCE CAN TOMATO PURÉE

1½ CUPS CHICKEN BROTH

1 FRESH JALAPEÑO PEPPER, SEEDED
 AND MINCED

6 CUPS STEAMED RICE

1. In a shallow bowl, mix together the flour, garlic, white pepper, cayenne pepper, 1 teaspoon of the thyme, and 1 teaspoon of the salt. Dredge the chicken in the seasoned flour. Set aside the remaining dredging flour.

2. Pour enough oil into a large skillet to measure ½ inch. Warm the oil over medium-high heat until very hot. Add the chicken, skin-side down, in batches if necessary, and fry until browned and crisp, 5 to 8 minutes on each side. Drain the chicken on paper towels.

3. Carefully pour the oil into a heatproof container. Return 2 tablespoons of the oil to the skillet. Add the reserved dredging flour and cook over high heat, stirring constantly, until the flour is golden brown, 30 seconds to 1 minute. Add the onions, red peppers, celery, leeks, tomatoes with their juice, tomato purée, broth, jalapeño pepper, and remaining ½ teaspoon thyme and ½ teaspoon salt. Cook the sauce for about 5 minutes, stirring occasionally. Reduce the heat to medium-low and simmer, partially covered, for 30 minutes.

4. Return the chicken to the skillet and simmer until heated through, 15 to 25 minutes. Serve the chicken and sauce hot over steamed rice.

VEGETABLE PIZZA

SERVES 8

♡ LOW-FAT

1 PACKAGE RAPID-RISE YEAST

1 TEASPOON SUGAR

½ CUP WARM WATER (120° TO 130°)

2 TEASPOONS OLIVE OIL

¾ CUP WHOLE-WHEAT FLOUR

¾ CUP ALL-PURPOSE FLOUR

1 TEASPOON SALT

1 CUP SMALL BROCCOLI FLORETS

1 CUP THINLY SLICED ZUCCHINI

1 CUP SLICED MUSHROOMS

1 CUP THINLY SLICED RED OR YELLOW
BELL PEPPER STRIPS

¼ CUP CHICKEN BROTH

2 CUPS COARSELY CHOPPED FRESH
SPINACH

½ CUP PIZZA SAUCE

¼ CUP GRATED PARMESAN CHEESE

1 CUP SKIM MILK MOZZARELLA CHEESE

1. In a small bowl, combine the yeast, sugar, water, and oil, and stir to combine.

2. In a medium bowl, combine the flours and salt. Add the yeast mixture and stir to form a soft dough. Transfer the dough to a floured surface and knead until the dough is smooth and elastic, about 5 minutes. Place the dough in a bowl oiled with vegetable or olive oil; cover and let rise until doubled in size, about 30 minutes.

3. In a large nonstick skillet combine the broccoli, zucchini, mushrooms, bell peppers, and broth, and cook over medium heat for 4 to 5 minutes, or until the liquid has evaporated. Stir in the spinach. Remove the skillet from the heat and set aside.

4. Preheat the oven to 425°. Spray a 12-inch pizza pan with nonstick cooking spray. On a lightly floured surface, roll the pizza dough into a 12-inch circle. Gently ease the dough into the prepared pan, pushing it out to the edges. Bake for 8 to 10 minutes, or until firm to the touch.

5. Remove the crust from the oven. Spread the pizza sauce over the crust. Sprinkle with 2 tablespoons of Parmesan cheese and ½ cup mozzarella. Spoon the vegetable mixture over the cheese. Sprinkle on the remaining mozzarella and Parmesan.

6. Bake the pizza for 15 to 17 minutes, or until the cheese is melted and the crust is browned. Cut into wedges with a pizza cutter.

Artichoke, Pepperoni, and Red Pepper Pizza

SERVES 8

3 CUPS FLOUR
1 PACKAGE RAPID-RISE YEAST
1 TEASPOON SALT
1 CUP WARM WATER (120° TO 130°)
2 TABLESPOONS VEGETABLE OIL
1 TABLESPOON CORNMEAL
1 CUP PIZZA SAUCE
2 CUPS MOZZARELLA CHEESE

TWO 6-OUNCE JARS ARTICHOKE
  HEARTS, DRAINED AND QUARTERED
4 OUNCES THINLY SLICED PEPPERONI
ONE 7-OUNCE JAR ROASTED RED
  PEPPERS, DRAINED AND COARSELY
  CHOPPED
2 TABLESPOONS CHOPPED FRESH BASIL
  OR 1 TEASPOON DRIED

1. In a medium bowl, combine 2 cups of flour, the yeast, and salt. Add the water and oil and stir, adding more flour as necessary to form a soft dough. Transfer the dough to a lightly floured surface and knead until the dough is smooth and elastic, about 5 minutes. Cover the dough with a kitchen towel and let rest on the floured surface for 10 minutes.

2. Preheat the oven to 425°. Lightly grease a 15 x 10-inch jelly-roll pan; sprinkle with the cornmeal.

3. With a floured rolling pin, roll the dough into a 15 x 10-inch rectangle. Gently ease the dough into the pan, pushing it out to the edges. Spread the pizza sauce over the dough; top with 1 cup of the mozzarella. Arrange the artichoke hearts, pepperoni, red peppers, and basil on top of the pizza. Sprinkle with the remaining cup of mozzarella.

4. Bake for 20 minutes, or until the crust is golden brown. Allow the pizza to rest 5 minutes before cutting into 8 wedges with a pizza cutter.

CHICKEN TETRAZZINI

S E R V E S   8

1 POUND BROAD EGG NOODLES	½ CUP SHERRY
1½ STICKS BUTTER	2 EGG YOLKS
½ POUND MUSHROOMS, THINLY SLICED	⅛ TEASPOON TABASCO SAUCE
6 TABLESPOONS FLOUR	2 CUPS COOKED CHICKEN, DICED
2 CUPS CHICKEN BROTH	1 CUP GRATED PARMESAN CHEESE
½ CUP HEAVY CREAM	

1. In a large pot of boiling water cook the noodles until al dente according to package directions. Drain the noodles in a colander and cool them under cold running water. Set aside.

2. In a medium skillet, melt 6 tablespoons of the butter over medium heat. Add the mushrooms and cook, stirring frequently, for about 5 minutes, or until they are soft and lightly colored. Remove from the heat and set aside.

3. In a medium saucepan, melt the remaining butter over medium heat. Stir in the flour and mix together thoroughly. Stirring the mixture constantly with a wire whisk, gradually pour in the broth, cream, and the sherry. Cook over high heat until the sauce comes to a boil, then reduce the heat to medium. In a small bowl, beat the egg yolks with a whisk.

Whisking constantly, slowly pour in about ½ cup of the hot liquid, then stir this egg mixture into the saucepan. Cook for an additional 1 to 2 minutes, then stir in the Tabasco sauce and remove the pan from the heat.

4. Preheat the oven to 350°. Grease the bottom and sides of a 9 x 13 x 2-inch baking dish.

5. Pour 1 cup of the sauce into the prepared baking dish and arrange half of the noodles over the sauce. Spread the noodles with half of the mushrooms, and top with half of the chicken. Repeat the layers using 1 cup of sauce and the remaining noodles, mushrooms, and chicken, and top with the remaining sauce. Sprinkle the sauce with the Parmesan cheese and bake for 30 minutes. Serve at once, directly from the baking dish.

Southwestern Tamale Pie

SERVES 6 TO 8

4 TABLESPOONS BUTTER

2 GARLIC CLOVES, MINCED

1 MEDIUM ONION, CHOPPED

1 POUND GROUND BEEF CHUCK

1 LARGE GREEN BELL PEPPER, CHOPPED

1 CUP CORN KERNELS, FRESH OR FROZEN

ONE 14-OUNCE CAN WHOLE TOMATOES, DRAINED

1 TABLESPOON TOMATO PASTE

2 TABLESPOONS CHILI POWDER

1 TEASPOON CUMIN

1½ TEASPOONS SALT

2½ CUPS MILK

¾ CUP YELLOW CORNMEAL

2 CUPS GRATED CHEDDAR CHEESE

¼ POUND PLUM TOMATOES, THINLY SLICED

½ CUP CHOPPED SCALLIONS

1. Preheat the oven to 350°. Grease a 2-quart casserole or soufflé dish.

2. In a large skillet, melt 2 tablespoons of the butter over medium-high heat. Add the garlic, onion, and ground beef, and cook, stirring occasionally, until the onion is softened and the beef begins to brown, about 10 minutes.

3. Stir in the green pepper, corn, canned tomatoes, tomato paste, chili powder, cumin, and 1 teaspoon of the salt. Reduce the heat to medium-low and simmer, uncovered, for about 10 minutes.

4. Meanwhile, in a medium saucepan, bring the milk almost to a boil over medium heat. Add the remaining 2 tablespoons butter and ½ teaspoon salt. Whisking constantly, gradually add the cornmeal. Reduce the heat to medium-low and simmer for 5 minutes. Remove from the heat and stir in 1 cup of the cheese.

5. Line the sides and bottom of the prepared casserole with two-thirds of the cornmeal mixture. Pour in the meat filling and top with the remaining cornmeal mixture, spreading it evenly. Sprinkle the remaining 1 cup cheese on top. Arrange the fresh tomato slices over the cheese. Bake, uncovered, for 40 minutes.

6. Sprinkle the scallions on top and bake for 5 minutes.

Oriental Chicken Salad

SERVES 8

⊕ EXTRA - QUICK

2 TABLESPOONS BUTTER

1½ CUPS SLIVERED ALMONDS

ONE 16-OUNCE PACKAGE COLESLAW
MIX

½ CUP SCALLIONS, CHOPPED

1 PACKAGE RAMEN-TYPE NOODLES,
UNCOOKED, BROKEN UP, RESERVING
FLAVOR PACKET FOR DRESSING

1 CUP COOKED CHICKEN, DICED

3 TABLESPOONS VINEGAR

1 TABLESPOON SUGAR

½ CUP VEGETABLE OIL

½ TEASPOON ORIENTAL (DARK) SESAME
OIL

¼ TEASPOON SALT

¼ TEASPOON PEPPER

ONE 11-OUNCE CAN MANDARIN
ORANGES, DRAINED

1. In a small skillet, melt the butter over low heat. Add the almonds and cook, shaking the pan, until the almonds are browned, about 3 to 5 minutes.

2. In a large bowl, toss together the almonds, coleslaw mix, scallions, ramen noodles, and chicken until combined.

3. In a small bowl, combine the vinegar, sugar, vegetable oil, sesame oil, salt, pepper, and the contents of the flavor packet, and mix well. Pour the dressing over the coleslaw mixture and toss to combine. Serve the salad garnished with the mandarin oranges.

Chicken Ratatouille

SERVES 8 TO 10

🕐 EXTRA-QUICK

3 TABLESPOONS FLOUR

¼ TEASPOON BLACK PEPPER

4 SKINLESS, BONELESS CHICKEN BREAST HALVES (ABOUT 1¼ POUNDS TOTAL), CUT INTO BITE-SIZE PIECES

3 TABLESPOONS OLIVE OIL

2 MEDIUM ONIONS, QUARTERED

4 GARLIC CLOVES, MINCED

ONE 14½-OUNCE CAN STEWED TOMATOES

PINCH OF SUGAR

½ SMALL EGGPLANT, CUT CROSSWISE INTO ¼-INCH SLICES

1 SMALL RED BELL PEPPER, CUT INTO SLIVERS

1 SMALL YELLOW SQUASH, HALVED LENGTHWISE AND CUT INTO ¼-INCH HALF-ROUNDS

¼ CUP CHOPPED FRESH BASIL OR 1½ TEASPOONS DRIED

1 TEASPOON OREGANO

1 SMALL ZUCCHINI, HALVED LENGTHWISE AND CUT INTO ¼-INCH HALF-ROUNDS

1. In a plastic bag, combine the flour and pepper and shake to mix. Add the chicken and shake to coat lightly. Remove the chicken, reserving the excess seasoned flour.

2. In a large saucepan, warm 2 tablespoons of the oil over medium-high heat. Add the chicken and cook until golden, about 5 minutes. Transfer the chicken to a plate.

3. Add the remaining 1 tablespoon oil, the onions, and garlic to the pan, and sauté until the mixture begins to brown, 3 to 5 minutes.

4. Add the reserved dredging mixture and stir until the flour is no longer visible. Add the tomatoes and sugar and bring to a boil. Add the eggplant, bell pepper, yellow squash, basil, and oregano, and return to a boil. Reduce the heat to medium-low, cover, and simmer until the vegetables are tender, 8 to 10 minutes.

5. Uncover and return the mixture to a boil over medium-high heat. Return the chicken (and any juices that have accumulated on the plate) to the saucepan and stir in the zucchini. Cook until the zucchini is just tender and the chicken is cooked through, about 2 minutes.

Spicy Beef Pasties

MAKES 12

2 CUPS FLOUR
⅔ CUP YELLOW CORNMEAL
½ CUP CHOPPED CILANTRO
1½ TEASPOONS SALT
6 TABLESPOONS BUTTER, AT ROOM
   TEMPERATURE
6 TABLESPOONS VEGETABLE
   SHORTENING
8 TO 10 TABLESPOONS ICE WATER
1 SMALL POTATO

½ POUND GROUND BEEF
1 MEDIUM CARROT, DICED
1 CUP CHOPPED SCALLIONS
3 GARLIC CLOVES, MINCED
ONE 4-OUNCE CAN DICED GREEN
   CHILIES, DRAINED
1½ TEASPOONS CUMIN
1 TEASPOON OREGANO, CRUMBLED
½ TEASPOON BLACK PEPPER
1 EGG, SLIGHTLY BEATEN

1. In a large bowl, combine the flour, cornmeal, ¼ cup of cilantro, and 1 teaspoon of salt. With a pastry blender or 2 knives, cut in the butter and shortening until the mixture is coarse crumbs. Sprinkle 8 tablespoons of ice water over the mixture and toss it with a fork until the dough can be formed into a cohesive ball. If necessary, add up to 2 tablespoons more ice water.

2. Peel and quarter the potato, then thinly slice each quarter. In a large bowl, combine the potato, ground beef, carrot, scallions, garlic, and green chilies. Add the remaining cilantro, cumin, oregano, salt, and pepper, and mix gently until well combined.

3. Preheat the oven to 375°. Line a baking sheet with foil and lightly grease the foil.

4. On a lightly floured surface, roll the dough out to a ¼-inch thickness. Using a saucer or a paper template, cut out twelve 5-inch rounds. Reroll and cut any scraps.

5. Spoon ¼ cup of filling onto 1 side of each pastry round, leaving a ½-inch border around the edge. Brush the edge of the pastry with water, then fold the pastry to cover the filling, forming semicircular turnovers. Seal the edges by pressing them with the tines of a fork.

6. Place the pasties on the prepared baking sheet, prick the tops with a fork, then brush them with the beaten egg. Bake for 30 to 35 minutes, or until the pasties are golden brown. Serve hot, or at room temperature.

Chicken Salad Sandwiches

SERVES 8

⏱ EXTRA-QUICK

2 CUPS FINELY CHOPPED COOKED
    CHICKEN

2 TABLESPOONS FINELY CHOPPED
    CELERY

1 TABLESPOON GRATED ONION

1 CUP FINELY CHOPPED TOASTED
    ALMONDS

½ TEASPOON CURRY POWDER

½ TEASPOON SALT

⅛ TEASPOON BLACK PEPPER

1 CUP MAYONNAISE

16 SLICES MULTI-GRAIN BREAD

8 ROMAINE LETTUCE LEAVES

1. In a medium bowl, combine the chicken, celery, onion, almonds, curry powder, salt, and pepper. Add the mayonnaise and mix thoroughly. Taste for seasoning.

2. Divide the chicken salad evenly among 8 slices of bread; top each with lettuce and another slice of bread.

KITCHEN NOTE: *You can use leftover home-cooked chicken for these sandwiches, or pick up some roast chicken at a deli or supermarket. Leftover turkey would also work well in this recipe.*

SEAFOOD SALAD SANDWICHES

SERVES 8

🕐 EXTRA-QUICK

1 POUND COOKED MEDIUM SHRIMP, COARSELY CHOPPED
½ POUND FRESH OR CANNED CRABMEAT
1 CUP CHOPPED CELERY
¼ CUP FINELY CHOPPED RED ONION
⅓ CUP MAYONNAISE
3 TABLESPOONS FRESH LEMON JUICE
2 TABLESPOONS CHOPPED FRESH DILL OR 2 TEASPOONS DRIED

¼ TEASPOON SALT
⅛ TEASPOON BLACK PEPPER
4 LARGE PITA BREADS, CUT IN HALF TO FORM 8 POCKETS
2 CUPS SHREDDED ROMAINE LETTUCE
1 SMALL CUCUMBER, PEELED AND THINLY SLICED

1. In a medium bowl, combine the shrimp, crabmeat, celery, and onion. In another medium bowl, whisk together the mayonnaise, lemon juice, dill, salt, and pepper until smooth and well blended. Stir the mayonnaise mixture into the shrimp and crabmeat until thoroughly combined.

2. For each sandwich, fill a pita half with ¼ cup of lettuce, ⅓ cup of the shrimp mixture, and a few cucumber slices.

VEGETABLE LASAGNA

SERVES 8

♡ LOW-FAT

1 TEASPOON OLIVE OIL

2 GARLIC CLOVES, CHOPPED

2 MEDIUM CARROTS, CUT INTO 1-INCH MATCHSTICKS

2 MEDIUM ZUCCHINI, CUT INTO 1-INCH MATCHSTICKS

10 OUNCES MUSHROOMS, THINLY SLICED

ONE 14½-OUNCE CAN ITALIAN-STYLE STEWED TOMATOES

ONE 8-OUNCE CAN TOMATO SAUCE

ONE 6-OUNCE CAN TOMATO PASTE

½ TEASPOON ITALIAN SEASONING

16 OUNCES LOW-FAT COTTAGE CHEESE

2 EGG WHITES

½ TEASPOON SALT

¼ TEASPOON BLACK PEPPER

8 OUNCES UNCOOKED LASAGNA NOODLES

½ CUP SKIM MILK MOZZARELLA CHEESE

½ CUP GRATED PARMESAN CHEESE

1. Preheat oven to 350°.

2. In a large saucepan, warm the oil over medium heat. Add the garlic and sauté for 1 minute. Add the carrots and zucchini and cook for 3 to 5 minutes, or until the vegetables are tender. Add the mushrooms, stewed tomatoes, tomato sauce, tomato paste, Italian seasoning, and 2 cups of water, and bring the mixture to a boil. Reduce the heat to low, cover, and simmer 5 minutes.

3. Meanwhile, in a medium bowl, combine the cottage cheese, egg whites, salt, and pepper, and stir until well blended.

4. Spoon 1½ cups of the vegetable sauce into a 13 x 9 x 2-inch baking dish, spreading evenly. Cover the sauce with a layer of noodles; spread the cottage cheese mixture on top. Top with half of the mozzarella and half of the Parmesan cheese. Again, layer with 1½ cups of the sauce and the remaining noodles. Top with the remaining sauce, mozzarella, and Parmesan cheese.

5. Cover the baking dish tightly with foil and bake for 45 minutes. Remove the foil and bake for 15 minutes to brown the cheese. Let the lasagna stand 15 minutes before cutting.

Ricotta-Stuffed Pasta Shells

SERVES 6 TO 8

24 JUMBO PASTA SHELLS

1½ POUNDS RICOTTA CHEESE

6 TABLESPOONS GRATED PARMESAN
  CHEESE

3 TABLESPOONS FINELY CHOPPED
  PARSLEY

1½ TEASPOONS GRATED LEMON ZEST

⅛ TEASPOON NUTMEG

1 TEASPOON SALT

¼ TEASPOON BLACK PEPPER

1 EGG YOLK

2 CUPS TOMATO SAUCE

1. In a large pot of boiling water, cook the pasta shells until al dente according to package directions.

2. In a large bowl, combine the ricotta, Parmesan, parsley, lemon zest, nutmeg, salt, pepper, and egg yolk. Beat vigorously until the filling is smooth.

3. Preheat the oven to 350°.

4. Stuff the cooled pasta shells evenly with the cheese mixture. Pour 1 cup of the tomato sauce into an ovenproof serving dish just large enough to hold the stuffed shells in one layer. Arrange the shells side by side in the dish, and pour the remaining cup of sauce over them. Bake for 15 to 20 minutes, or until the sauce bubbles. Serve hot.

Substitution: *Ricotta cheese is finer grained than cottage cheese, with a mildly sweet flavor. If necessary, you can substitute cottage cheese; drain the cheese in a strainer for a few minutes to remove any excess liquid before adding the seasonings and egg yolk.*

CALZONES

SERVES 8

2 PACKAGES ACTIVE DRY YEAST
6 CUPS FLOUR
1 TEASPOON SALT
1 TEASPOON BLACK PEPPER
1 POUND RICOTTA CHEESE
1 POUND GOAT CHEESE, CRUMBLED
4 GARLIC CLOVES, MINCED

2 TABLESPOONS MINCED PARSLEY
4 TABLESPOONS MINCED FRESH BASIL
1 POUND MOZZARELLA CHEESE,
   SHREDDED
½ CUP OLIVE OIL
2 CUPS TOMATO SAUCE, HEATED

1. Preheat the oven to 500°. Grease a large baking sheet with vegetable oil.

2. In a large bowl, combine 2 cups of hot tap water with the yeast and stir to dissolve.

3. Add the flour, salt, and pepper, and stir until the dough forms a ball. Test the consistency of the dough by squeezing a small portion of it in your hand. If it sticks to your palm, knead in a bit more flour until the dough is no longer sticky; if the dough is too dry, add water, 1 tablespoon at a time, and knead until the dough is smooth and elastic. Let the dough rise in the bowl for 10 minutes.

4. In a medium bowl, combine the ricotta and goat cheese and blend with a fork. Stir in the garlic, parsley, and basil. Gently fold in the mozzarella.

5. Transfer the dough to a lightly floured surface and knead it briefly. Pat the dough into a ball and divide it into eighths. Roll out each piece of dough into an 8-inch circle about ⅛ inch thick.

6. Place ⅛ of the filling on the lower half of each circle, leaving a 1-inch border. Brush the edges of the dough with cold water and fold the top half of the circle over the filling. Fold the border back to double-seal the dough; crimp the edges with the tines of a fork.

7. Transfer the calzones to the prepared baking sheet and brush with the olive oil. Bake for 15 minutes, or until puffed and golden. Serve the calzones with tomato sauce.

Italian Meatballs

SERVES 6 TO 8

2 SLICES ITALIAN BREAD, TORN INTO
SMALL PIECES

½ CUP MILK

1 EGG, LIGHTLY BEATEN

1 POUND GROUND BEEF

¼ POUND SWEET ITALIAN SAUSAGE,
REMOVED FROM CASING

6 TABLESPOONS GRATED PARMESAN
CHEESE

2 TABLESPOONS CHOPPED PARSLEY

1 TABLESPOON OLIVE OIL

2 TEASPOONS FINELY CHOPPED GARLIC

1 TEASPOON GRATED LEMON ZEST

¼ TEASPOON ALLSPICE

1 TEASPOON SALT

PINCH OF BLACK PEPPER

¼ CUP VEGETABLE OIL

24 OUNCES TOMATO SAUCE

1. Soak the pieces of bread in the milk for 5 minutes, then squeeze them dry and discard the milk. In a large bowl, combine the soaked bread, the beaten egg, beef, sausage, cheese, parsley, olive oil, garlic, lemon zest, allspice, salt, and pepper. Knead the mixture vigorously with both hands or beat with a wooden spoon until all of the ingredients are well blended.

2. Shape the mixture into small balls about 1½ inches in diameter. Lay the meatballs out in one layer on a baking sheet, cover them with plastic wrap and chill for at least 1 hour.

3. Warm the vegetable oil in a large skillet until hot. Cook the meatballs 5 or 6 at a time over medium-high heat, shaking the pan constantly to roll the balls and help keep them round. Cook the meatballs for 8 to 10 minutes, or until they are brown on the outside and show no trace of pink inside. Add more vegetable oil to the skillet as it is needed. Drain the meatballs on paper towels.

4. In a large pot, warm the tomato sauce over medium heat. Add the meatballs to the sauce and cook until heated through.

STUFFED PEPPERS

SERVES 8

2 TABLESPOONS OLIVE OIL

4 TABLESPOONS BUTTER

3 CUPS FRESH WHITE BREAD CRUMBS

2 TEASPOONS FINELY CHOPPED GARLIC

ONE 2-OUNCE CAN FLAT ANCHOVY
 FILLETS, RINSED AND FINELY
 CHOPPED (OPTIONAL)

6 TABLESPOONS CAPERS, RINSED IN
 COLD WATER AND FINELY CHOPPED

8 BLACK OLIVES, PITTED AND FINELY
 CHOPPED

4 TABLESPOONS FINELY CHOPPED
 PARSLEY

½ TEASPOON SALT

¼ TEASPOON BLACK PEPPER

4 LARGE GREEN BELL PEPPERS, CUT IN
 HALF LENGTHWISE, SEEDS REMOVED

1. Preheat the oven to 400°. Pour the oil into a shallow baking dish large enough to hold the green pepper halves comfortably. Tip the dish back and forth to spread the oil evenly across the bottom.

2. In a medium skillet, melt the butter over medium heat. Add the bread crumbs and cook, stirring constantly, until they are crisp and lightly browned. Remove the skillet from the heat and stir in the garlic. Then add the anchovies (if using), capers, olives, and parsley, and mix well. Stir in the salt and pepper and taste for seasoning. If the stuffing mixture looks too dry and crumbly, moisten it with a little olive oil.

3. Spoon the stuffing into the pepper halves and arrange them in the oiled baking dish. Bake for about 30 minutes, or until the peppers are tender but not limp and the stuffing is lightly browned on top. Serve hot or cold.

Ham and Seafood Jambalaya

SERVES 8

1 CUP SHORT-GRAIN RICE

2 TABLESPOONS VEGETABLE OIL

2 MEDIUM ONIONS, CHOPPED

3 GARLIC CLOVES, MINCED

ONE 35-OUNCE CAN WHOLE TOMATOES

2 CELERY RIBS, CHOPPED

1 MEDIUM GREEN BELL PEPPER, DICED

¼ CUP CHOPPED PARSLEY

½ TEASPOON HOT PEPPER SAUCE

1 TEASPOON THYME

⅛ TEASPOON CAYENNE PEPPER

1 BAY LEAF

1 TEASPOON SALT

½ TEASPOON BLACK PEPPER

½ POUND HAM, CUT INTO ½-INCH CUBES

1 PINT SHUCKED OYSTERS, DRAINED

1 POUND MEDIUM SHRIMP, SHELLED AND DEVEINED

1. In a medium saucepan, bring 2 cups of water to a boil. Add the rice. Reduce the heat to low, cover, and simmer until the rice is tender, about 20 minutes. Fluff the rice with a fork, cover, and set aside.

2. In a Dutch oven or flameproof casserole, warm the oil over medium heat. Add the onions and garlic, and sauté until the onions are softened but not browned, about 10 minutes. Add the tomatoes with their juice, breaking them up with the back of a spoon, and simmer for 5 minutes.

3. Add the celery, bell pepper, 2 tablespoons of the parsley, the hot pepper sauce, thyme, cayenne pepper, bay leaf, salt, and black pepper. Cook, stirring frequently, until the vegetables are tender, 25 to 30 minutes.

4. Add the ham and oysters and cook, stirring, for 5 minutes. Add the shrimp and cook until they just turn pink, 3 to 4 minutes.

5. Add the rice and cook, stirring, until the jambalaya is heated through and the rice has absorbed any liquid in the pan. Remove and discard the bay leaf.

6. Garnish the jambalaya with the remaining 2 tablespoons of parsley and serve.

Chicken and Sausage Gumbo

SERVES 6 TO 8

½ CUP FLOUR

1 TEASPOON PAPRIKA

1 TEASPOON SALT

½ TEASPOON BLACK PEPPER

¼ TEASPOON CAYENNE PEPPER

2½ POUNDS CHICKEN PARTS

3 TABLESPOONS VEGETABLE OIL

2 MEDIUM ONIONS, CHOPPED

3 GARLIC CLOVES, MINCED

2 CELERY RIBS, CHOPPED

1 TEASPOON THYME

1 TEASPOON WORCESTERSHIRE SAUCE

5 CUPS CHICKEN BROTH

½ POUND KIELBASA, OR OTHER GARLIC
SAUSAGE, CUT INTO ½-INCH
ROUNDS

TWO 10-OUNCE PACKAGES FROZEN
OKRA

1 MEDIUM YELLOW OR GREEN BELL
PEPPER, CUT INTO 1-INCH SQUARES

6 CUPS STEAMED RICE

2 TABLESPOONS CHOPPED PARSLEY

1. In a shallow bowl, combine the flour, paprika, salt, black pepper, and cayenne pepper. Dredge the chicken in the seasoned flour. Reserve the excess dredging flour.

2. In a Dutch oven or flameproof casserole, warm the oil over medium-high heat. Add the chicken, skin-side down, and cook until golden brown, 2 to 3 minutes per side. Drain the chicken on paper towels.

3. Pour off all but 3 tablespoons of fat and warm over medium-high heat. Add the onions and garlic and sauté, stirring frequently, until the onions begin to brown, about 5 minutes. Add the reserved dredging flour and cook, stirring constantly, until the flour turns dark brown, 2 to 3 minutes.

4. Add the celery, thyme, Worcestershire sauce, broth, and kielbasa. Increase the heat to high and bring to a boil, stirring frequently. Add the chicken, reduce the heat to medium-low, cover, and simmer for 40 minutes or, until the chicken is tender.

5. Remove the chicken and, when it is cool enough to handle, remove the meat from the bones. Cut the meat into cubes and return it to the gumbo. Add the okra and bell pepper. Increase the heat to medium-high, bring to a boil, and cook for 5 minutes.

6. Serve the gumbo over rice, sprinkled with parsley.

BEEF TACOS

MAKES 8

EXTRA-QUICK

1 TABLESPOON OLIVE OIL

1 CUP FINELY CHOPPED ONIONS

1 TEASPOON FINELY CHOPPED GARLIC

1 POUND LEAN GROUND BEEF

1 TEASPOON CRUMBLED DRIED
   OREGANO

½ TEASPOON CUMIN

1 TEASPOON SALT

8 TACO SHELLS

1 CUP SHREDDED CHEDDAR CHEESE

1 CUP CHOPPED TOMATOES

1 CUP FINELY SHREDDED ICEBERG
   LETTUCE

1 CUP TACO SAUCE

1. In a large skillet, warm the oil over medium heat. Add the onions and garlic and cook for 5 minutes, or until the onions begin to soften. Add the beef, oregano, cumin, and salt, and cook for 8 to 10 minutes, stirring frequently and breaking up the meat with the back of a spoon, until no pink remains.

2. Preheat the oven to 350°.

3. Spoon the beef filling into the taco shells, dividing it evenly among them. Arrange the tacos upright in a baking dish just large enough to hold them. Bake for 10 minutes.

4. Dividing evenly, fill each taco with cheese, tomatoes, lettuce, and the remaining onions. Serve immediately with the taco sauce on the side.

VARIATION: *For soft tacos, warm 8 small flour tortillas in a dry skillet or in the microwave until they are pliable. Divide the beef mixture, cheese, tomatoes, lettuce, and reserved onions among the tortillas and fold them in half over the filling. Cook the tacos, a few at a time, in a large, lightly greased skillet over medium heat until the tortillas are lightly browned. Serve with the taco sauce.*

CHICKEN FAJITAS WITH RED PEPPERS

MAKES 20

1 CUP FRESH LEMON JUICE
½ CUP OLIVE OIL
1 CUP CHOPPED CILANTRO
6 GARLIC CLOVES, MINCED
3 TEASPOONS OREGANO
5 TEASPOONS BASIL
1 TEASPOON SALT
½ TEASPOON BLACK PEPPER

3 POUNDS SKINLESS, BONELESS
    CHICKEN BREAST HALVES
5 RED BELL PEPPERS, THINLY SLICED
20 FLOUR TORTILLAS
2 LARGE RED ONIONS, THINLY SLICED
3 CUPS SOUR CREAM
4 CUPS PITTED SMALL BLACK OLIVES
10 CUPS SHREDDED ROMAINE LETTUCE

1. In a large bowl, combine the lemon juice, oil, cilantro, garlic, oregano, basil, salt, and pepper. Add the chicken and bell peppers and toss until well coated with the marinade. Cover the bowl with plastic wrap and marinate for at least 4 hours, or overnight, in the refrigerator, tossing a few times if possible.

2. Preheat the broiler. Line a large broiler pan with foil.

3. Working in batches, place the chicken breasts and bell peppers on the broiler pan and broil 4 to 6 inches from the heat for 4 to 6 minutes per side, or until the chicken is cooked through and the peppers are limp. Wrap each batch of chicken and bell peppers in foil to keep it warm.

4. Meanwhile, stack the tortillas, wrap in foil, and warm them in a 200° oven.

5. Cut the chicken on the diagonal into thin strips. Present the chicken, bell peppers, and tortillas on warm serving platters with the onions, sour cream, olives, and lettuce in small bowls on the side for the guests to fill and roll their own fajitas.

ROAST LEG OF LAMB
WITH MINT SAUCE

SERVES 8

1 TABLESPOON SUGAR

¼ CUP FINELY CHOPPED FRESH MINT
LEAVES

½ CUP MALT VINEGAR

2 TABLESPOONS SALT

1 TEASPOON BLACK PEPPER

1 TABLESPOON FINELY CHOPPED FRESH
ROSEMARY OR 2 TEASPOONS DRIED

5- TO 6-POUND LEG OF LAMB

1. In a small saucepan, combine ¼ cup of water and the sugar and bring to a boil over high heat, stirring until the sugar dissolves completely.

2. Remove the pan from the heat, and stir in the mint leaves and vinegar. Taste and add up to 1 more tablespoon of sugar, if desired. Set the mint sauce aside at room temperature for 2 to 3 hours.

3. Preheat the oven to 500°.

4. In a small bowl, combine the salt, pepper, and rosemary. Press the mixture firmly into the lamb, coating the entire surface as evenly as possible.

5. Place the leg, fat-side up, on a rack in a shallow pan, and roast it, uncovered, for 20 minutes.

6. Reduce the oven temperature to 375° and roast for another 40 to 60 minutes, or until the lamb is cooked to your taste. A meat thermometer inserted into the thickest part of the leg will register 130° to 140° for rare, 140° to 150° for medium, and 150° to 160° for well done.

7. Transfer the lamb to a heated platter, and let rest for 15 minutes for easier carving. Stir the mint sauce once or twice, pour it into a sauceboat, and serve it separately with the lamb.

STUFFED ROAST TURKEY

SERVES 8 TO 10

1 POUND PORK SAUSAGE
2 TABLESPOONS PLUS 1 STICK BUTTER
4 CELERY RIBS, CHOPPED
1 RED APPLE, UNPEELED AND CUBED
1 MEDIUM ONION, CHOPPED
1 GARLIC CLOVE, MINCED
½ CUP CHICKEN BROTH
1 CUP RAISINS

16 SLICES FIRM-TEXTURED BREAD, CUBED
¼ CUP CHOPPED PARSLEY
1 TEASPOON SAGE
2½ TEASPOONS SALT
1½ TEASPOONS BLACK PEPPER
ONE 12-POUND TURKEY

1. Preheat the oven to 425°.

2. In a large skillet, cook the sausage over medium heat for 10 minutes, breaking it up with a wooden spoon. Add 2 tablespoons of butter, the celery, apple, onion, garlic, and broth, and cook for 10 minutes. Add the raisins, bread, parsley, sage, and ½ teaspoon each of salt and pepper, and stir to combine.

3. Stuff the turkey loosely and truss with a needle and thread. Blend 6 tablespoons of butter with the remaining salt and pepper, and rub the outside of the turkey with the seasoned butter. Place the turkey, breast-side up, in a roasting pan and roast until golden brown, 30 to 35 minutes. In a small saucepan, melt the remaining 2 tablespoons of butter.

4. Turn the turkey on its side, baste with the pan juices, and brush with 1 tablespoon of melted butter. Reduce the oven temperature to 350° and roast for 45 minutes, basting after 20 minutes. Turn the turkey onto its other side, baste with the pan juices, and brush with the remaining tablespoon melted butter. Roast for another 45 minutes, basting after about 20 minutes. Should any portion of the turkey seem to be browning too quickly, cover it loosely with foil.

5. The turkey is done when a meat thermometer inserted into the thickest part of the leg (but not touching the bone) measures 180°. If it is not done, roast it, breast-side up, for another 20 minutes, continuing to baste, and check again. Remove the turkey from the oven and transfer the stuffing to a large serving bowl. (For safety reasons, do not leave any stuffing in the turkey.) Let the turkey rest at least 15 minutes before carving.

SIDE DISHES AND SALADS

Boston Baked Beans

SERVES 6 TO 8

4 CUPS GREAT NORTHERN BEANS
3 MEDIUM ONIONS, PEELED
2 TEASPOONS SALT
4 CLOVES
½ CUP MOLASSES

1 CUP BROWN SUGAR
2 TEASPOONS DRY MUSTARD
1 TEASPOON BLACK PEPPER
½ POUND SALT PORK, SCORED

1. Put the beans in a large saucepan and pour in enough cold water to cover them by at least 2 inches. Bring to a boil, let boil for 2 minutes, then let the beans soak in the water off the heat for about 1 hour. Bring them to a boil again. Add 1 onion and 1 teaspoon of the salt. Half cover the pan and simmer the beans as slowly as possible for about 30 minutes, or until they are partially done. Drain the beans and discard the bean water and the onion.

2. Preheat the oven to 250°.

3. Place 2 onions, each stuck with 2 cloves, in the bottom of a 2½-quart bean pot or casserole and cover with the beans.

4. In a small bowl, combine the molasses, ¾ cup of the brown sugar, the dry mustard, and 1 teaspoon each of salt and pepper. Slowly stirring with a large spoon, pour in 2 cups of water. Pour the mixture over the beans and push the pork slightly beneath the surface.

5. Cover tightly and bake for 4½ to 5 hours. Remove the cover and sprinkle with the remaining ¼ cup of brown sugar. Bake the beans, uncovered, for another ½ hour and serve.

SCALLOPED POTATOES

SERVES 8 TO 10

4 POUNDS ALL-PURPOSE POTATOES,
   PEELED AND CUT INTO ¼-INCH
   SLICES
2 TABLESPOONS BUTTER
2 LARGE ONIONS, COARSELY CHOPPED
1 CUP DICED HAM OR CANADIAN
   BACON
2 TABLESPOONS FLOUR

2½ CUPS MILK
½ CUP HEAVY CREAM
2 CUPS GRATED SHARP CHEDDAR
   CHEESE
½ TEASPOON SALT
¼ TEASPOON BLACK PEPPER
1 TEASPOON WORCESTERSHIRE SAUCE
½ TEASPOON DRY MUSTARD

1. Preheat the oven to 375°. Grease a 13 x 9 x 2-inch baking dish. Cook the potatoes in a large pot of boiling water for 4 to 5 minutes, or until almost tender; drain and set aside.

2. In a medium saucepan, melt the butter over medium heat. Add the onions and ham and cook, stirring, for 4 to 5 minutes, or until the onions are softened. Stir in the flour and cook for 1 minute. Remove the pan from the heat and stir in the milk and cream. Return the pan to the stove and bring to a boil over medium heat, stirring, until the mixture bubbles and thickens, about 2 to 3 minutes.

3. Stir in 1½ cups of the cheese, the salt, pepper, Worcestershire sauce, and dry mustard, and cook for about 1 minute, or until the cheese is melted.

4. Layer one-third of the potatoes in the bottom of the prepared pan. Pour one-third of the sauce over the potatoes. Repeat twice with the remaining potatoes and sauce. Sprinkle the remaining cheese over the top.

5. Bake for 30 to 35 minutes, or until the potatoes are tender and the top is golden brown.

TWICE-BAKED POTATOES WITH SPINACH AND CHEESE

MAKES 16 HALVES

8 LARGE IDAHO BAKING POTATOES

2 TABLESPOONS BUTTER

1 LARGE ONION, CHOPPED

ONE 10-OUNCE PACKAGE CHOPPED
FROZEN SPINACH, THAWED AND
DRAINED

¾ TEASPOON SALT

¼ TEASPOON BLACK PEPPER

¼ TEASPOON NUTMEG

1 CUP SOUR CREAM

2 CUPS GRATED SWISS CHEESE

1. Preheat the oven to 450°. Pierce each potato 2 or 3 times and place on a baking sheet. Bake the potatoes for 50 to 60 minutes, or until tender when pierced with a fork.

2. In a medium saucepan, melt the butter over medium heat. Add the onion and cook, stirring, for 4 to 5 minutes, or until the onion has softened. Stir in the spinach, salt, pepper, and nutmeg. Cook for 1 minute, or until heated through.

3. Cut each baked potato in half lengthwise. Scoop the flesh out into a medium bowl, leav-

ing a ¼-inch shell. With a fork or a potato masher, mash the potatoes. Stir in the sour cream, the onion-spinach mixture, and 1½ cups of Swiss cheese until well blended.

4. Spoon the potato mixture into the potato shells. Sprinkle the remaining Swiss cheese over the filling. Place the stuffed potatoes on 2 baking sheets. Bake for 15 minutes, or until the potatoes are heated through and the cheese is melted.

Broccoli and Cheddar Casserole

10 SLICES FIRM-TEXTURED WHITE
BREAD, CRUSTS TRIMMED AND
BREAD CUT INTO CUBES

3 CUPS BROCCOLI FLORETS AND STEMS

2 CUPS GRATED EXTRA-SHARP
CHEDDAR CHEESE

5 EGGS, BEATEN

2½ CUPS MILK

1 TEASPOON WORCESTERSHIRE SAUCE

½ TEASPOON DRY MUSTARD

½ TEASPOON SALT

1 MEDIUM ONION, CHOPPED

¼ POUND BACON (4 TO 6 SLICES)

1. Grease a 9 x 13 x 2-inch baking dish.

2. Spread half of the bread cubes on the bottom of the prepared baking dish. Alternate layers of broccoli, cheese, and bread, ending with cheese.

3. In a medium bowl, combine the eggs, milk, Worcestershire sauce, mustard, salt, and onion. Pour the mixture over the ingredients in the baking dish. Cover and refrigerate for 6 hours, or overnight.

4. Preheat the oven to 350°.

5. Bake the casserole, uncovered, for 1 hour, or until a knife inserted in the center comes out clean. Let the casserole stand 10 minutes before cutting.

6. Meanwhile, in a large skillet, cook the bacon over medium heat until crisp, about 10 minutes. Drain on paper towels and crumble.

7. Serve the casserole topped with the crumbled bacon.

Pasta Primavera

SERVES 8

2 CUPS OF BROCCOLI, CUT INTO BITE-
SIZE PIECES

2 SMALL ZUCCHINI, HALVED AND CUT
INTO ¼-INCH SLICES

2 MEDIUM CARROTS, CUT DIAGONALLY
INTO ¼-INCH SLICES

½ CUP FROZEN PEAS

½ MEDIUM RED BELL PEPPER, CUT INTO
THIN STRIPS

4 TABLESPOONS OLIVE OIL

8 OUNCES MUSHROOMS, SLICED

3 GARLIC CLOVES, FINELY CHOPPED

3½ CUPS CHOPPED TOMATO

¼ CUP CHOPPED PARSLEY

¼ CUP CHOPPED FRESH BASIL OR
2 TEASPOONS DRIED

16 OUNCES PENNE PASTA

4 TABLESPOONS BUTTER

⅔ CUP HEAVY CREAM

¾ CUP GRATED PARMESAN CHEESE

½ TEASPOON SALT

¼ TEASPOON BLACK PEPPER

1. Cook the broccoli, zucchini, and carrots in a pot of salted boiling water for 3 to 5 minutes, or until the vegetables are just tender but still crisp. Add the peas and red pepper and cook for 1 minute. Drain and rinse the vegetables under cold water; set aside.

2. In a large skillet, warm the oil over medium heat. Add the mushrooms and cook for 2 minutes. Add the garlic and tomatoes and cook for 5 minutes. Stir in the parsley and basil.

3. In a large pot of boiling water, cook the penne until al dente or according to package directions. Drain and set aside.

4. In a large saucepan, melt the butter. Add the cream and Parmesan and bring to a boil, stirring constantly. When the mixture begins to boil, remove from the heat and stir until smooth. Add the vegetables and the tomato-mushroom mixture, stirring until blended.

5. Transfer the contents of the saucepan to a large bowl. Add the penne, salt, and pepper, and toss gently to combine. Transfer the mixture back to the saucepan and cook over low heat until heated through. Serve hot.

Seven-Vegetable Chili

SERVES 10 TO 12

♡ LOW-FAT

4 TABLESPOONS OLIVE OIL

1 MEDIUM RED ONION, COARSELY CHOPPED

4 GARLIC CLOVES, MINCED

3 CUPS CANNED PINTO BEANS, RINSED AND DRAINED

2 CUPS CAULIFLOWER FLORETS

1 MEDIUM SWEET POTATO, PEELED AND DICED

1 LARGE GREEN BELL PEPPER, DICED

2 LARGE CARROTS, DICED

3 CUPS FRESH OR FROZEN CORN KERNELS

ONE 35-OUNCE CAN WHOLE TOMATOES

1 CUP CHICKEN BROTH

3 TABLESPOONS CUMIN

3 TABLESPOONS CHILI POWDER

2 TABLESPOONS TOMATO PASTE

2 TEASPOONS PAPRIKA

1½ TEASPOONS SALT

⅛ TEASPOON CAYENNE PEPPER

¼ CUP CHOPPED CILANTRO

1. In a Dutch oven or flameproof casserole, heat 2 tablespoons of the oil over medium heat. Add the onion and garlic and sauté until the onion is softened but not browned, about 10 minutes.

2. Add the remaining 2 tablespoons of oil to the pan, then add the beans, cauliflower, sweet potato, bell pepper, carrots, corn, tomatoes, broth, cumin, chili powder, tomato paste, paprika, salt, and cayenne pepper, and stir until well combined. Bring to a boil over medium-high heat, then reduce the heat to medium-low and simmer, covered, stirring frequently, until the vegetables are just tender, about 10 minutes. For more tender vegetables, cook the chili for another 20 minutes.

3. Just before serving, stir in the cilantro.

KITCHEN NOTE: *A Dutch oven is a large, heavy pot with a tight-fitting lid. Because it can be used on the stovetop or in the oven, it's very useful for cooking soups, stews, pot roasts, and the like.*

VEGETABLE PILAF

SERVES 6 TO 8

4 TABLESPOONS VEGETABLE OIL
1 CUP FINELY CHOPPED ONIONS
2 CUPS IMPORTED BASMATI RICE OR
   OTHER LONG-GRAIN WHITE RICE
2 CUPS FRESH GREEN BEANS, CUT INTO
   2-INCH LENGTHS, OR 2 CUPS
   FROZEN GREEN BEANS, THAWED
2 MEDIUM CARROTS, CUT INTO
   ⅛-INCH-THICK SLICES

1 MEDIUM GREEN BELL PEPPER, CUT
   INTO THIN STRIPS
1 MEDIUM POTATO, PEELED AND CUT
   INTO ½-INCH CUBES
1 CUP FRESH GREEN PEAS, OR 1 CUP
   FROZEN PEAS, THAWED
4 CUPS CHICKEN BROTH
2 TABLESPOONS FINELY CHOPPED FRESH
   CORIANDER OR CILANTRO

1. In a large saucepan, warm the oil over medium heat until hot. Add the onions and sauté for 7 to 8 minutes, stirring constantly, until the onions are soft and golden brown. Watch carefully for any sign of burning and regulate the heat accordingly.

2. Stir in the rice and, when the mixture is well combined, add the beans, carrots, green pepper, potato, peas, and broth. Stirring frequently, bring to a boil over high heat and boil for 5 minutes, then reduce the heat to low.

3. Cover the saucepan and simmer for 20 minutes, or until the rice and vegetables are tender and all the liquid in the pan has been absorbed.

4. To serve, mound the pilaf on a heated platter and sprinkle the top with coriander.

Wild Rice with Mushrooms and Pecans

SERVES 6

4 TABLESPOONS BUTTER

2 TABLESPOONS FINELY DICED CARROTS

2 TABLESPOONS FINELY DICED CELERY

2 TABLESPOONS FINELY CHOPPED
  ONION

1 CUP WILD RICE

1 TEASPOON SALT

2 CUPS CHICKEN BROTH

½ POUND MUSHROOMS, COARSELY
  CHOPPED

2 TABLESPOONS FINELY CHOPPED
  PARSLEY

¼ CUP FINELY CHOPPED PECANS

1. In a medium saucepan, warm 2 tablespoons of the butter over medium heat until melted. Add the carrots, celery, and onions, cover, and cook for 10 to 15 minutes, stirring occasionally, until the vegetables are soft but not brown. Stir in the rice and the salt and cook for 2 to 3 minutes, uncovered, stirring to coat the rice thoroughly with the butter.

2. In a small saucepan, bring the broth to a boil and pour it over the rice. Bring to a boil again, cover tightly, and reduce the heat to low. Cook undisturbed for 25 to 30 minutes, or until the rice is tender and has absorbed all the liquid.

3. Meanwhile, in a medium skillet, melt the remaining 2 tablespoons of butter over medium heat. Add the mushrooms and parsley; cook, stirring, for 5 minutes. Add the pecans and cook for 2 to 3 minutes. With a fork, stir the contents of the skillet into the finished rice. Taste for seasoning and serve.

SPICED COUSCOUS

SERVES 8

⏲ EXTRA-QUICK

1 TABLESPOON VEGETABLE OIL

1 LARGE ONION, CHOPPED

2 LARGE CARROTS, DICED

1 GARLIC CLOVE, MINCED

1 TEASPOON CUMIN

¼ CUP GOLDEN RAISINS

ONE 13¾-OUNCE CAN CHICKEN BROTH

½ TEASPOON SALT

ONE 12-OUNCE PACKAGE COUSCOUS

¼ CUP CHOPPED PARSLEY

1. In a large saucepan, warm the oil over medium heat. Add the onion, carrots, and garlic and cook, stirring, until the onion and carrots have softened, about 5 minutes.

2. Stir in the cumin and cook 1 minute. Add the raisins, broth, salt, and 1¾ cups of water.

Increase the heat to high and bring the mixture to a boil. Stir in the couscous. Reduce the heat to low, cover, and cook for 2 minutes.

3. Remove the pan from the heat and let stand for 3 minutes. Stir in the parsley and serve.

KITCHEN NOTE: *Couscous, which looks like tiny beads of grain, is a North African pasta; it is made, like Italian pastas, from semolina flour. The type of couscous sold in most supermarkets is "instant" or "quick-cooking" and can be cooked like pasta or by steeping it in boiling water. Try this exotic side dish where you'd ordinarily serve mashed potatoes or rice—for example, with roast chicken and gravy, braised pork chops, or lamb curry.*

Potato Rolls

MAKES 10

♡ LOW-FAT

ONE ¼-POUND WHITE OR SWEET
POTATO
1 CUP BUTTERMILK
1 CUP DARK RAISINS
2 TABLESPOONS VEGETABLE OIL

2 TABLESPOONS SUGAR
1 PACKAGE ACTIVE DRY YEAST
3¼ CUPS FLOUR
2 TABLESPOONS NONFAT DRY MILK
PINCH OF SALT

1. Place the potato in a small saucepan with cold water to cover, and bring to a boil over medium heat. Cover the pan, reduce the heat to medium-low, and cook the potato 20 minutes, or until tender when pierced with a fork. When the potato is cooked, set it aside to cool slightly; reserve the cooking water.

2. Peel the potato, mash it in a small bowl, then stir in the buttermilk, raisins, and oil; set aside.

3. In a small bowl, combine ¼ cup of the warm cooking water and 1 tablespoon of sugar. Add the yeast and let the mixture stand 1 to 2 minutes, or until the yeast begins to foam. Meanwhile, in a medium bowl, combine the flour, dry milk, the remaining sugar, and the salt and make a well in the center. Pour in the potato and yeast mixtures and stir until well combined.

4. Turn the dough onto a lightly floured surface and knead for 5 to 7 minutes, or until smooth, dusting it with more flour if necessary to prevent sticking. Place the dough in a clean medium bowl, cover it with a kitchen towel, and set aside in a warm place to rise for 40 minutes, or until doubled in size.

5. Punch down the dough and knead it on a floured surface 1 minute. Roll it into a 20-inch-long rope about 2 inches thick, cut the rope into 10 sections and place them on a baking sheet. Set aside to rise in a warm place for 25 minutes.

6. Preheat the oven to 350°.

7. Bake the rolls for 15 to 20 minutes, or until golden brown on top. Let cool slightly before serving.

CORNMEAL BISCUITS

MAKES 16

♡ LOW-FAT

2 CUPS FLOUR
⅔ CUP YELLOW CORNMEAL
1 TABLESPOON SUGAR
2 TEASPOONS BAKING POWDER

PINCH OF SALT
3 TABLESPOONS BUTTER
¾ CUP SKIM MILK

1. Preheat the oven to 425°.

2. In a medium bowl, combine the flour, cornmeal, sugar, baking powder, and salt, and stir to blend. Transfer the mixture to a food processor.

3. Cut the butter into small pieces, add it to the food processor and process, pulsing the machine on and off, about 10 seconds, or until the mixture is coarse meal. Add the milk, and process another 10 seconds, or until the dough forms a cohesive mass. To mix the dough by hand, cut the butter into the dry ingredients with a pastry blender or 2 knives, then add the milk and stir until combined.

4. Transfer the dough to a lightly floured surface and knead it gently for 30 seconds, or just until smooth. Roll out the dough with a floured rolling pin to a ¾-inch thickness.

5. With a floured 2-inch biscuit cutter, cut out 16 biscuits and place them on a baking sheet. Bake for 10 minutes, or until golden. Serve warm.

THREE-BEAN SALAD

SERVES 6 TO 8

1 CUP CANNED RED KIDNEY BEANS,
   RINSED AND DRAINED
1 CUP CANNED WHITE KIDNEY BEANS,
   RINSED AND DRAINED
1 CUP CANNED CHICK PEAS, RINSED
   AND DRAINED
¾ CUP FINELY CHOPPED ONION OR
   SCALLIONS
½ TEASPOON FINELY CHOPPED GARLIC

2 TABLESPOONS FINELY CHOPPED
   PARSLEY
1 SMALL GREEN BELL PEPPER,
   COARSELY CHOPPED
1 TEASPOON SALT
PINCH OF BLACK PEPPER
3 TABLESPOONS RED WINE VINEGAR
½ CUP OLIVE OIL

1. In a large bowl, combine the red kidney beans, white kidney beans, chick peas, onion, garlic, parsley, and green pepper.

2. Add the salt, pepper, and vinegar. Toss gently with a large spoon. Pour in the oil and toss again. Let the salad rest for an hour before serving.

VARIATION: *"Three-Bean" isn't a hard-and-fast rule: You can add other canned beans (black, pinto, black-eyed peas) in any combination to equal three cups. Or add a cup of cooked, cut-up green beans or yellow wax beans, or thawed frozen corn kernels.*

POTATO SALAD
WITH BACON BITS

SERVES 6 TO 8

3 POUNDS MEDIUM BOILING POTATOES
½ POUND BACON
½ CUP FINELY CHOPPED ONIONS
¼ CUP WHITE WINE OR CIDER VINEGAR
½ TEASPOON SALT

¼ TEASPOON BLACK PEPPER
1 TEASPOON DRY MUSTARD
2 TABLESPOONS FINELY CHOPPED FRESH
    CHIVES OR SCALLION GREENS

1. Drop the potatoes into enough lightly salted boiling water to cover them completely, and boil briskly, uncovered, until they show only slight resistance when pierced with the point of a sharp knife. Do not overcook. Drain the potatoes in a colander, peel and cut them into ¼-inch-thick slices. Set aside in a large bowl and cover tightly with foil.

2. In a medium skillet, cook the bacon over medium heat until brown and crisp. Transfer the bacon to paper towels to drain.

3. Add the onions to the pan and stir over medium heat until they are soft and golden. Add the vinegar, salt, pepper, mustard, and ¼ cup of water, and bring the sauce to a boil. Pour the hot sauce over the potatoes, turning to coat evenly. Crumble in the bacon, add the chives, and stir gently to combine. Serve the potato salad immediately.

Cucumber and Sour Cream Salad

SERVES 6

4 MEDIUM CUCUMBERS, PEELED AND
  CUT INTO ¼-INCH-THICK SLICES
1 TABLESPOON COARSE SALT, OR
  2 TABLESPOONS TABLE SALT
½ TEASPOON DISTILLED WHITE
  VINEGAR
3 HARD-BOILED EGGS
1 TEASPOON DIJON MUSTARD

⅓ CUP SOUR CREAM
2 TEASPOONS WHITE WINE VINEGAR
¼ TEASPOON SUGAR
⅛ TEASPOON WHITE PEPPER
4 TO 6 LARGE LETTUCE LEAVES
1 TABLESPOON FINELY CHOPPED FRESH
  DILL

1. In a medium bowl, combine the cucumber slices, salt, and vinegar, and toss until the cucumber is well moistened. Marinate at room temperature for 30 minutes, then drain the cucumbers through a sieve and pat them thoroughly dry with paper towels. Place them in a large bowl.

2. Separate the yolks from the whites of the hard-boiled eggs. Cut the whites into ⅛-inch-wide strips. Stir the egg whites into the cucumber.

3. With the back of a large spoon, rub the egg yolks through a sieve set over a small bowl. Slowly beat in the mustard, sour cream, white wine vinegar, sugar, and white pepper. When the dressing is smooth, pour it over the cucumbers and toss together gently but thoroughly. Taste for seasoning.

4. To serve, arrange the lettuce leaves on a large flat serving plate or on small individual plates and mound the salad on top of them. Sprinkle with dill and refrigerate until ready to serve.

Spinach Salad

SERVES 4 TO 6

🕐 EXTRA-QUICK

½ POUND FRESH SPINACH, STEMMED

1 LARGE CUCUMBER, HALVED
LENGTHWISE AND CUT INTO ¼-INCH
HALF-CIRCLES

4 MEDIUM CELERY RIBS, DICED

¼ CUP COARSELY CHOPPED BLACK
OLIVES

½ CUP PINE NUTS

2 TABLESPOONS RED WINE VINEGAR

½ TEASPOON SALT

BLACK PEPPER

½ TEASPOON DRY MUSTARD

6 TABLESPOONS OLIVE OIL

1. In a large salad bowl, toss the spinach, cucumber, and celery. Add the olives and nuts and toss again. Chill until ready to serve.

2. For the dressing, with a whisk, beat the vinegar, salt, pepper, and mustard together in a small bowl. Still whisking, gradually pour in the oil and beat until the dressing is smooth and thick.

3. Just before serving, pour the dressing over the salad and toss until all the ingredients are thoroughly coated with the dressing.

Substitution: *For a big flavor boost, use tangy kalamata or niçoise or other brine-cured olives. Gourmet shops, Middle Eastern groceries, and some supermarket deli departments offer a wide variety of olives in bulk; don't hesitate to ask for samples.*

CAESAR SALAD

SERVES 4 TO 6

🕐 EXTRA-QUICK

2 HEADS OF ROMAINE LETTUCE, TORN
    INTO BITE-SIZE PIECES
4 TO 8 TABLESPOONS VEGETABLE OIL
4 SLICES FIRM-TEXTURED FRENCH OR
    ITALIAN BREAD, CUBED
1 TEASPOON FINELY CHOPPED GARLIC
1 HARD-BOILED EGG

1 TEASPOON MAYONNAISE
⅛ TEASPOON SALT
⅛ TEASPOON BLACK PEPPER
½ CUP OLIVE OIL
4 TABLESPOONS FRESH LEMON JUICE
1 CUP GRATED PARMESAN CHEESE
6 TO 8 FLAT ANCHOVIES (OPTIONAL)

1. Place the lettuce in a salad bowl and refrigerate until ready to serve.

2. In a large skillet, warm 4 tablespoons of the vegetable oil over high heat until a light haze forms above it. Add the bread cubes and brown them on all sides, turning them with tongs, and, if necessary, add up to another 3 tablespoons of oil. Remove the pan from the heat, then add the chopped garlic and toss the croutons about in the hot fat. Transfer the croutons to paper towels to drain.

3. Remove the white from around the egg yolk and discard. In a small bowl, mash the egg yolk. Add the mayonnaise, salt, pepper, olive oil, lemon juice, and Parmesan, and whisk vigorously until well combined.

4. Just before serving, pour the dressing over the lettuce and toss to combine. Scatter the anchovies (if using) and the croutons over the top and serve.

TABBOULEH SALAD

SERVES 6 TO 8

⏱ EXTRA-QUICK

½ CUP BULGUR

3 MEDIUM TOMATOES, FINELY CHOPPED

1 CUP FINELY CHOPPED PARSLEY

1 CUP FINELY CHOPPED ONIONS

⅓ CUP FRESH LEMON JUICE

2 TEASPOONS SALT

⅓ CUP OLIVE OIL

2 TABLESPOONS FINELY CHOPPED FRESH MINT OR 1 TABLESPOON DRIED MINT, CRUMBLED

ROMAINE LETTUCE LEAVES (OPTIONAL)

1. Place the crushed wheat in a medium bowl and pour in enough cold water to cover it completely. Let it soak for about 10 minutes, then drain in a sieve or colander lined with a double thickness of dampened cheesecloth. Wrap the crushed wheat in the cheesecloth and squeeze it vigorously until it is completely dry.

2. Drop the crushed wheat into a large bowl. Add the tomatoes, parsley, onions, lemon juice, and salt, and toss gently but thoroughly together with a fork.

3. Just before serving, stir in the olive oil and mint and taste for seasoning. Mound the salad in a serving bowl lined with Romaine lettuce leaves, if desired.

KITCHEN NOTE: *Cracked wheat (which comes in a presteamed form called bulgur) is a staple in the Middle East, especially in Syria and Lebanon. Tabbouleh, a very popular dish made from it, makes a refreshing warm-weather meal. Serve it with pita bread.*

BRUNCHES

Banana Pancakes
with Strawberry Sauce

SERVES 8

♡ LOW-FAT

2 CUPS STRAWBERRIES

1 TABLESPOON PLUS ¼ CUP SUGAR

1 TEASPOON CORNSTARCH

1 EGG

1½ CUPS BUTTERMILK

1 CUP MASHED BANANA

½ CUP SKIM MILK

1⅔ CUPS FLOUR

2 TEASPOONS BAKING SODA

1 TEASPOON BAKING POWDER

1 TEASPOON CINNAMON

1. In a medium saucepan, combine the strawberries, 1 tablespoon of the sugar, and 2 teaspoons of water. Cover and cook over medium-low heat for 10 minutes, or until the strawberries are tender. Increase the heat to medium-high and bring the mixture to a boil.

2. Meanwhile, stir together the cornstarch and 2 teaspoons of water in a cup. Add this mixture to the sauce and cook 1 minute, or until thickened. Remove the pan from the heat and mash the strawberries with a fork. Cover the pan to keep warm and set aside.

3. In a medium bowl, beat together the egg, buttermilk, banana, and milk; set aside.

4. In a large bowl, stir together the flour, the remaining sugar, the baking soda, baking powder, and cinnamon, and make a well in the center. Add the egg mixture and stir until well blended.

5. Spray a large nonstick skillet with nonstick cooking spray and heat it over medium-high heat. Pour in four ¼-cup portions of batter and spread them with a spoon to form 5-inch pancakes. Cook the pancakes 2 minutes, or until bubbles appear on the tops and the bottoms are golden. Turn the pancakes and cook another 2 minutes, or until the second side is golden. Transfer the pancakes to a plate and cover them with foil to keep warm. Continue making more pancakes in the same fashion.

6. Serve the pancakes with the strawberry sauce on the side.

BLUEBERRY BUTTERMILK PANCAKES

SERVES 6 TO 8

♡ LOW-FAT

1¼ CUPS FLOUR
1 CUP CORNMEAL
1½ TEASPOONS BAKING SODA
1 TEASPOON BAKING POWDER
PINCH OF SALT
2¼ CUPS BUTTERMILK

2 EGGS, SEPARATED, PLUS 1 EGG
   WHITE
3 TABLESPOONS BROWN SUGAR
2 CUPS FRESH OR UNSWEETENED
   FROZEN BLUEBERRIES, THAWED
1 TABLESPOON VEGETABLE OIL

1. In a small bowl, stir together the flour, cornmeal, baking soda, baking powder, and salt; set aside.

2. In a large bowl, whisk together the buttermilk, egg yolks, and sugar; set aside.

3. In another large bowl, with an electric mixer, beat the egg whites until stiff peaks form.

4. Add the flour mixture to the buttermilk mixture and stir until blended, then gently fold in the egg whites. Stir in the blueberries.

5. Heat ½ teaspoon of oil in a large nonstick skillet over medium heat. Using ¼ cup of batter for each pancake, make 4 pancakes, cooking them about 4 minutes on each side, or until golden brown. Make 5 more batches of pancakes in the same fashion, adding ½ teaspoon of oil to the skillet before cooking each batch.

Raisin Waffles with Fruit Sauce

SERVES 6 TO 8

♡ LOW-FAT

1 CUP DICED FRESH PINEAPPLE

½ CUP DRIED APRICOTS, CUT INTO
½-INCH STRIPS

1 CUP GOLDEN RAISINS

2 CINNAMON STICKS

1 TEASPOON GRATED LIME ZEST

2 TABLESPOONS MAPLE SYRUP

2 CUPS FLOUR

3 TEASPOONS SUGAR

1½ TEASPOONS BAKING POWDER

¼ TEASPOON BAKING SODA

2 EGGS, SEPARATED

½ CUP BUTTERMILK

3 TABLESPOONS BUTTER, MELTED AND
COOLED

¼ CUP SHREDDED UNSWEETENED
COCONUT

1. In a medium saucepan, stir together the pineapple, apricots, ½ cup of the raisins, the cinnamon sticks, lime zest, and ¾ cup of water. Cover and bring the sauce to a boil, then reduce the heat and simmer, stirring occasionally, for 30 minutes. Stir in the maple syrup.

2. Meanwhile, in a large bowl, stir together the flour, sugar, baking powder, and baking soda, and set aside.

3. In a medium bowl, whisk together the egg yolks, buttermilk, and butter until well blended.

4. In another large bowl, beat the egg whites until stiff peaks form.

5. Add the buttermilk mixture to the flour mixture and stir until blended, then stir in the remaining raisins. With a rubber spatula, fold in the egg whites.

6. Preheat a nonstick waffle iron. (If your waffle iron does not have a nonstick surface, spray it with nonstick cooking spray before heating it.) Pour in some batter, spread it evenly with a rubber spatula, and bake 2 to 3 minutes, or until the waffle is browned and crisp. Continue to make more waffles in the same fashion. (Do not respray the hot iron.)

7. Serve the waffles topped with the fruit sauce and sprinkled with coconut.

FRENCH TOAST WAFFLES

SERVES 8

♡ LOW-FAT

4 EGGS, BEATEN
2 CUPS SKIM MILK
1 TEASPOON GROUND CINNAMON

16 SLICES RAISIN BREAD
½ CUP UNSWEETENED APPLE BUTTER

1. Preheat a nonstick waffle iron. (If your waffle iron does not have a nonstick surface, spray it with nonstick cooking spray before heating it.)

2. In a shallow bowl, beat together the eggs, milk, and cinnamon. Dip the bread in the egg mixture, turning it to coat both sides.

3. Place the bread in the waffle iron and cook it 2 minutes, or until golden brown. Continue to make more waffles in the same fashion. (Do not respray the hot iron.)

4. Serve the french toast waffles with the apple butter on the side.

VARIATION: *Apple butter is just one option for topping this nifty waffled toast. Here's another: Heat fresh or frozen blueberries until they begin to soften and burst. Sweeten a bit, if necessary, and add a little cinnamon, vanilla extract, and lemon zest to taste.*

French Toast Fingers with Apple Purée

SERVES 6

4 GRANNY SMITH APPLES, PEELED AND
  THINLY SLICED
1 CUP APPLE JUICE
1 TEASPOON FRESH LEMON JUICE
PINCH OF GRATED LEMON ZEST
PINCH OF PUMPKIN-PIE SPICE
⅔ CUP GOLDEN RAISINS
¼ CUP CHOPPED WALNUTS

3 LARGE EGGS PLUS 4 EGG WHITES
3 TABLESPOONS SKIM MILK
1 TEASPOON VANILLA EXTRACT
¼ TEASPOON CINNAMON
1 TABLESPOON PLUS 2 TEASPOONS
  VEGETABLE OIL
12 SLICES WHOLE-WHEAT BREAD, EACH
  CUT INTO 4 STRIPS

1. In a medium saucepan over medium heat, cook the apples, apple juice, lemon juice, lemon zest, and pumpkin-pie spice for 10 minutes. Transfer the mixture to a food processor or blender and process until puréed but still chunky. Stir in the raisins and walnuts. Return the purée to the pan and cover to keep warm.

2. In a large, shallow bowl, whisk together the eggs, egg whites, and milk. Add the vanilla and cinnamon; set aside.

3. In a large nonstick skillet, heat 2 teaspoons of oil over medium-high heat. Dip 16 strips of bread into the egg mixture, place them in the skillet and cook 3 minutes. Turn the toast and cook another 3 minutes, or until well browned. Dip and cook the remaining bread in the same fashion, adding more oil as necessary.

4. Serve the french toast fingers with the apple purée on the side.

Orange-Nutmeg Pan Toast

SERVES 8

♡ LOW-FAT

2 EGGS

1 CUP SKIM MILK

2 TEASPOONS GRATED ORANGE ZEST

½ TEASPOON NUTMEG

16 SLICES FRENCH BREAD,
  ½ INCH THICK

½ CUP MAPLE SYRUP

2 TABLESPOONS POWDERED SUGAR

1. Place the eggs, milk, 2 tablespoons of water, the orange zest, and nutmeg in a large shallow dish, and whisk to combine.

2. Place the bread slices in the egg mixture to coat 1 side, then immediately turn the bread. Let the bread stand at least 10 minutes.

3. Warm the syrup in a small saucepan.

4. Heat a nonstick griddle or nonstick skillet over medium heat. Brown both sides of the bread slices on the griddle or in the skillet. Sprinkle with powdered sugar and serve with the warm syrup.

KITCHEN NOTE: *If you make straight crosswise cuts in a loaf of French bread, you'll end up with small, round pieces. Instead, cut the bread on a long diagonal to make large slices.*

BLUEBERRY CREPES

SERVES 8

♡ LOW-FAT

1 CUP FLOUR

3 TABLESPOONS SUGAR

3 LARGE EGGS

2 CUPS FROZEN UNSWEETENED
   BLUEBERRIES, THAWED AND DRAINED

2 ORANGES, PEELED, HALVED, AND CUT
   CROSSWISE INTO THIN SLICES

2 TABLESPOONS HONEY

2 TABLESPOONS FRESH LEMON JUICE

¼ TEASPOON CARDAMOM

1 TABLESPOON VEGETABLE OIL

1. In a food processor or blender, combine, the flour, sugar, eggs, and 1½ cups of water, and process 1 minute. Transfer the batter to a bowl, cover, and refrigerate until needed. (The batter can be made up to 3 hours in advance.)

2. For the filling, combine the blueberries, orange slices, honey, lemon juice, and cardamom in a medium saucepan, and cook over medium heat 5 minutes, or until the fruit is slightly softened.

3. Preheat the oven to 200°.

4. To make the crepes, stir the batter well to reblend it. Heat a medium nonstick skillet over medium-high heat and brush it lightly with oil. Pour in ¼ cup of batter and swirl the pan to coat the bottom evenly. Cook the crepe 1½ minutes, then turn it and cook another 30 seconds. Transfer the cooked crepe to a heatproof plate, cover it loosely with foil and place it in the oven to keep warm. Repeat to make a total of 8 crepes.

5. Reserve ½ cup of filling. To assemble the crepes, lay each, browned-side down, on a small plate, spoon about ¼ cup of filling on top and fold the sides of the crepe over the filling. Top each crepe with a spoonful of the remaining filling.

VEGGIE-CHEESE EGG BAKE

SERVES 8

2 TABLESPOONS BUTTER

1 LARGE ONION, DICED

2 CUPS CHOPPED MUSHROOMS

2 CUPS COARSELY CHOPPED BROCCOLI,
BLANCHED

12 LARGE EGGS

½ CUP FLOUR

1 TEASPOON SALT

½ TEASPOON BLACK PEPPER

2 CUPS COTTAGE CHEESE

2 CUPS SHREDDED SWISS CHEESE

1. Preheat the oven to 375°. Grease a 13 x 9 x 2-inch baking dish.

2. In a large nonstick skillet, melt the butter over medium-high heat. Add the onions and cook, stirring, for 4 to 5 minutes, or until the onions are softened. Add the mushrooms and broccoli and cook, stirring, for 5 minutes, or until the mushrooms are tender. Remove the skillet from the heat and set aside to cool.

3. Meanwhile, in a large bowl, beat the eggs with a whisk. Beat in the flour, salt, and pepper. Stir in the cottage cheese and Swiss cheese until well blended. Stir in the cooked vegetables. Pour the mixture into the prepared baking dish. Bake for 35 to 40 minutes, or until set in the center.

4. Let cool for 5 minutes before cutting into 8 squares.

VARIATION: *Add ¼ cup crumbled crisp bacon or finely diced cooked smoked ham to the egg mixture; or substitute blanched asparagus, cut into 1-inch pieces, for the broccoli.*

Italian Frittata

SERVES 8

2 TABLESPOONS OLIVE OIL

1 POUND SWEET OR HOT ITALIAN
   SAUSAGE, CRUMBLED

1 RED BELL PEPPER, DICED

1 GREEN BELL PEPPER, DICED

1 LARGE ONION, CHOPPED

2 GARLIC CLOVES, MINCED

10 LARGE EGGS

½ CUP GRATED PARMESAN CHEESE

1 TEASPOON ITALIAN SEASONING

¾ TEASPOON SALT

1. In a 12-inch cast-iron or ovenproof skillet, warm 1 tablespoon of the oil over medium heat. Add the sausage and cook, stirring, until browned and cooked through, about 6 to 7 minutes. Transfer the sausage to paper towels to drain.

2. Add the remaining tablespoon of oil to the drippings in the skillet. Add the peppers, onions, and garlic and cook over medium heat for 5 to 6 minutes, or until the onions are softened.

3. In a large bowl, beat the eggs with a whisk. Stir in the Parmesan, Italian seasoning, and salt. Return the cooked sausage to the skillet and stir to mix thoroughly.

4. Pour the egg mixture over the sausage and peppers in the skillet. Reduce the heat to medium-low and cook, covered, for 13 to 15 minutes, or until the egg mixture is almost set.

5. Preheat the broiler.

6. Place the skillet under the broiler 6 to 7 inches from the heat and cook for 3 to 4 minutes, or until the eggs are completely set in the center. Let the frittata rest for 2 to 3 minutes before cutting it into 8 wedges.

Zucchini and Cheese Quiche

SERVES 8

4 MEDIUM ZUCCHINI, SLICED
1¼ CUPS FLOUR
½ TEASPOON SALT
6 TABLESPOONS PLUS 1 TEASPOON
   BUTTER
3 TO 4 TABLESPOONS ICE WATER
1 MEDIUM ONION, FINELY CHOPPED

1½ TABLESPOONS CHOPPED FRESH
   BASIL OR 1½ TEASPOONS DRIED
4 OUNCES CAMEMBERT CHEESE, RIND
   REMOVED, CUT INTO SMALL PIECES
1¼ CUPS MILK
2 EGGS, BEATEN
PINCH OF BLACK PEPPER

1. Preheat the oven to 350°. Put the zucchini into a lightly oiled baking dish. Cover the dish with foil and bake about 20 minutes, or until the zucchini is tender.

2. Meanwhile, in a large bowl, combine the flour and ¼ teaspoon of the salt. With a pastry blender or 2 knives, cut 6 tablespoons of the butter into the flour until the mixture is fine crumbs. Stir in 3 to 4 tablespoons of ice water to make a firm dough.

3. Transfer the dough to a floured surface and knead until smooth. Roll the dough out to a 12-inch circle. Transfer the dough to a 9-inch quiche dish or pie plate. Trim the dough to a 1-inch overhang; crimp the edges to form a decorative border. Prick the bottom and sides of the pastry shell with a fork, then chill for 20 minutes. Meanwhile, increase the oven temperature to 400°.

4. Bake the pastry shell for 15 minutes, then remove it from the oven and set it aside. Lower the oven temperature to 350°.

5. In a medium skillet, melt the remaining butter over medium heat. Add the onion and sauté until it is translucent, about 5 minutes. Add the basil and cook for 1 minute.

6. Spread half of the onion mixture in the bottom of the quiche shell and cover it with half of the zucchini, then add the remaining onions, followed by the rest of the zucchini. Sprinkle the cheese on top.

7. In a medium bowl, whisk together the milk, eggs, and pepper, and the remaining salt. Pour the egg mixture over the layered vegetables. Bake the quiche until it is set and golden brown, about 30 to 40 minutes. Allow the quiche to cool to room temperature before cutting it into wedges and serving.

Huevos Rancheros

SERVES 8

1 TABLESPOON VEGETABLE OIL

1 LARGE ONION, CHOPPED

1 GARLIC CLOVE, MINCED

3 LARGE TOMATOES, DICED

ONE 4-OUNCE CAN CHOPPED GREEN
   CHILIES, DRAINED

1 TEASPOON SALT

½ TEASPOON SUGAR

2 TABLESPOONS CHOPPED CILANTRO OR
   PARSLEY

EIGHT 6-INCH CORN TORTILLAS

12 LARGE EGGS, LIGHTLY BEATEN

⅓ CUP LIGHT CREAM

¼ TEASPOON BLACK PEPPER

2 TABLESPOONS BUTTER

1 CUP GRATED MONTEREY JACK OR
   PEPPER JACK CHEESE

1 MEDIUM AVOCADO, PEELED AND CUT
   INTO 16 SLICES

1. Preheat the oven to 350°.

2. In a medium saucepan, warm the oil over medium heat. Add the onions and garlic and cook, stirring, until the onions are softened. Add the tomatoes, chilies, ½ teaspoon of salt, and the sugar. Reduce the heat to low and cook, covered, for 5 minutes, stirring occasionally, until the sauce has thickened. Stir in the cilantro.

3. Meanwhile, wrap the tortillas in foil and warm in the oven until heated through, about 5 to 6 minutes.

4. In a large bowl, combine the eggs, cream, the remaining salt, and the pepper. In a large skillet, melt the butter over medium heat. Stir in the egg mixture and cook, gently stirring, until the eggs begin to thicken, about 4 to 5 minutes. Remove the skillet from the heat and stir in the cheese.

5. For each serving, arrange 1 warm tortilla on a plate; top with some of the scrambled eggs and tomato-chili sauce and 2 slices of avocado. Serve immediately.

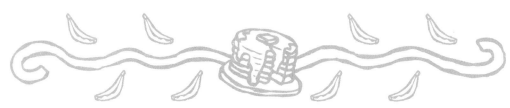

GLAZED PEACH COFFEECAKE

SERVES 6

½ CUP SLICED ALMONDS

2 PEACHES, UNPEELED

3 TABLESPOONS FRESH LEMON JUICE

⅓ CUP BUTTER, AT ROOM
    TEMPERATURE

⅓ CUP SUGAR

2 EGGS

⅓ CUP MILK

1 TEASPOON ALMOND EXTRACT

1 TEASPOON GRATED LEMON ZEST

1¾ CUPS FLOUR

1½ TEASPOONS BAKING POWDER

¼ TEASPOON SALT

3 TABLESPOONS APRICOT JAM

POWDERED SUGAR, FOR DUSTING

1. Preheat the oven to 375°. Grease and flour an 11 x 7-inch pan.

2. In a small nonstick skillet, toast the almonds over medium heat until golden, about 7 minutes.

3. Cut one of the peaches into ½-inch wedges. Toss the wedges with the lemon juice to keep them from discoloring. Finely chop the second peach.

4. In a large bowl, cream the butter and sugar until light and fluffy. Beat in the eggs, milk, almond extract, and lemon zest.

5. In a medium bowl, thoroughly combine the flour, baking powder, and salt. Add the dry ingredients to the mixing bowl and stir just until the dry ingredients are no longer visible. Fold in the toasted almonds and the chopped peach.

6. Spread the batter evenly into the prepared pan. Rap the pan once or twice on the counter to remove any air pockets. Arrange the peach wedges in 2 parallel rows about ¾ inch apart so the batter can rise between them. Bake for about 25 minutes, or until the top is golden and the cake pulls away from the sides of the pan. Cool the cake in the pan on a rack for 20 to 30 minutes.

7. In a small saucepan, warm the jam over low heat until melted, about 5 minutes. Spoon or brush a small amount of melted jam over each peach slice. Dust the top of the cake with powdered sugar.

Mini Apple-Walnut Coffeecakes

SERVES 8

¼ CUP MILK

2 TEASPOONS FRESH LEMON JUICE

1 LARGE APPLE, UNPEELED

3 QUARTER-SIZE SLICES FRESH GINGER, UNPEELED

1 STICK BUTTER

⅓ CUP BROWN SUGAR

1 EGG

1 TEASPOON VANILLA EXTRACT

1¼ CUPS FLOUR

½ TEASPOON BAKING POWDER

½ TEASPOON BAKING SODA

¼ TEASPOON SALT

¼ CUP RAISINS

¼ CUP CHOPPED WALNUTS

¼ CUP POWDERED SUGAR

1. Preheat the oven to 425°. Grease and flour an extra-large muffin tin or line the cups with paper liners.

2. In a small bowl, combine the milk with ½ teaspoon of the lemon juice and set aside.

3. Core and quarter the apple. In a food processor, finely chop the ginger. Add the apple quarters and coarsely chop. Transfer the ginger-apple mixture to a plate or bowl and set aside.

4. In the same processor work bowl (it does not need to be rinsed out), cream the butter and brown sugar. Add the egg and pulse just to combine. Add the soured milk and the vanilla and pulse to combine.

5. In a small bowl, thoroughly combine the flour, baking powder, baking soda, and salt. Add the flour mixture to the processor and pulse briefly, just until the flour is no longer visible. Fold the ginger-apple mixture, raisins, and walnuts into the batter.

6. Spoon the batter into the muffin tin and bake for about 25 minutes, or until a toothpick inserted in the center of a cake comes out clean. Cool the cakes in the tin on a rack for 15 minutes, then turn them out of the tin.

7. Meanwhile, in a small bowl, combine the powdered sugar with the remaining 1½ teaspoons lemon juice. Drizzle the glaze over the cooled cakes.

Blueberry Muffins

MAKES 20

2½ CUPS FRESH OR FROZEN
    BLUEBERRIES
2 CUPS FLOUR
2 TEASPOONS BAKING POWDER
½ TEASPOON SALT

1 STICK BUTTER
1 CUP SUGAR
2 EGGS
½ CUP MILK

1. Preheat the oven to 375°. Grease 20 muffins cups or line with paper liners.

2. In a medium bowl, combine the blueberries with 2 tablespoons of the flour. Toss to coat evenly.

3. In another medium bowl, combine the remaining flour, the baking powder, and salt.

4. In a large bowl, cream the butter and sugar until light and fluffy. Beat in the eggs, 1 at a time, beating well after each addition.

5. Alternating between the 2, beat in flour mixture and the milk, beating well after each addition. Fold in the floured blueberries.

6. Spoon the batter into the prepared muffin cups, filling each cup about ¾ full. Bake in the middle of the oven for 20 to 25 minutes, or until a toothpick inserted into the center of a muffin comes out clean. Turn the muffins out of the tins to cool slightly. Serve warm.

KITCHEN NOTE: *If you're baking first thing in the morning you won't have time to let the butter soften. Here's the solution: Cut the butter into thick pats and microwave it on medium-low for 30 seconds, or just until softened. Or, grate the butter on a hand grater.*

Corn Muffins

MAKES 1 DOZEN

⏱ EXTRA - QUICK   ♡ LOW - FAT

½ CUP BUTTERMILK

1 TABLESPOON PLUS 1 TEASPOON
BUTTER, MELTED AND COOLED

1 EGG, LIGHTLY BEATEN

½ CUP YELLOW CORNMEAL

⅓ CUP FLOUR

¼ CUP BROWN SUGAR

2 TEASPOONS BAKING POWDER

PINCH OF SALT

1. Preheat the oven to 375°. Grease and flour 12 muffin tin cups or line with paper liners.

2. In a medium bowl, stir together the buttermilk, butter, and egg until blended.

3. In another medium bowl, combine the cornmeal, flour, sugar, baking powder, and salt. Add the cornmeal mixture to the buttermilk mixture and stir just to combine; do not overmix.

4. Divide the batter among the muffin tin cups and bake 20 minutes, or until the muffins are golden brown and a toothpick inserted into the center of a muffin comes out clean.

KITCHEN NOTE: *There are two basic types of cornmeal. Stone-ground (also called water-ground) retains bits of the corn germ and hull; it's more nutritious and more flavorful than the finer steel-ground meal. Both types of cornmeal are available at most stores. Keep stone-ground cornmeal in the refrigerator or freezer.*

CRANBERRY-ORANGE BREAD

2 CUPS CRANBERRIES, COARSELY CHOPPED

1 MEDIUM APPLE, FINELY CHOPPED

½ CUP FINELY CHOPPED WALNUTS

2 CUPS FLOUR

1 CUP SUGAR

1½ TEASPOONS BAKING POWDER

½ TEASPOON BAKING SODA

¼ TEASPOON SALT

6 TABLESPOONS BUTTER, AT ROOM TEMPERATURE

1 EGG, LIGHTLY BEATEN

1 TABLESPOON GRATED ORANGE ZEST

½ CUP FRESH ORANGE JUICE

1. Preheat the oven to 350°. Grease and flour the bottom and sides of a 9 x 5-inch loaf pan.

2. In a medium bowl, combine the cranberries, apple, and walnuts; set aside.

3. In a large bowl, combine the flour, sugar, baking powder, baking soda, and salt. With a pastry blender or 2 knives, cut the butter into the flour mixture until it is coarse crumbs. Stir in the egg, orange zest, and orange juice until combined; do not overmix. Gently fold in the fruit-nut mixture.

4. Spread the batter evenly into the prepared pan. Bake for 1½ hours, or until the top is golden brown and a toothpick inserted into the center of the loaf comes out clean.

5. Turn the loaf out onto a rack to cool. Serve the bread warm or at room temperature.

DATE-NUT BREAD

MAKES ONE 9-INCH LOAF

8 OUNCES PITTED DATES, CHOPPED
½ CUP FINELY CHOPPED PECANS
4 TEASPOONS GRATED ORANGE ZEST
2 TABLESPOONS PLUS 2 CUPS FLOUR
1 TEASPOON BAKING POWDER
1 TEASPOON BAKING SODA

1 TEASPOON SALT
4 TABLESPOONS BUTTER
1 CUP SUGAR
1 EGG
1 CUP MILK

1. Preheat the oven to 350°. Grease and flour the bottom and sides of a 9 x 5-inch loaf pan.

2. In a small bowl, combine the dates, pecans, and orange zest. Add 2 tablespoons of the flour and toss to coat.

3. In a medium bowl, combine the remaining 2 cups of flour, the baking powder, baking soda, and salt. Set aside.

4. In a large bowl, cream the butter and sugar until light and fluffy. Beat in the egg until well combined. Alternating between the 2, beat in the flour mixture and the milk, beating well after each addition. Stir in the floured fruit and nuts.

5. Pour the batter into the prepared pan and bake for 50 to 60 minutes, or until a toothpick inserted into the center of the bread comes out clean. Let the bread cool in the pan for 4 to 5 minutes, then turn it out onto a rack to cool completely.

Buttermilk-Raisin Scones

MAKES 6

🕐 EXTRA-QUICK ♡ LOW-FAT

2 CUPS FLOUR

2 TEASPOONS BAKING POWDER

2 TABLESPOONS SUGAR

3 TABLESPOONS BUTTER, AT ROOM
TEMPERATURE

½ CUP RAISINS

1 TEASPOON GRATED ORANGE ZEST

¾ CUP BUTTERMILK

1. Preheat the oven to 425°. Spray a baking sheet with nonstick cooking spray.

2. In a medium bowl, combine the flour, baking powder, and sugar. With a pastry blender or 2 knives, cut the butter into the flour mixture until it is coarse crumbs. Scatter in the raisins and orange zest, then with a fork, stir in the buttermilk until just combined. Transfer the dough to a floured surface and knead 5 times.

3. Divide the dough into 6 equal portions and shape each into a ball. Place the balls of dough on the baking sheet. With a sharp knife cut a cross in the top of each. Bake the scones about 15 minutes, or until golden brown. Serve warm.

Variation: *Other kinds of dried fruit, such as currants or chopped apricots, may be substituted for the raisins. For a distinctly untraditional variation, you could use chocolate chips.*

BACON-CHEDDAR BISCUITS

MAKES 1 DOZEN

3 SLICES BACON
2 CUPS FLOUR
2 TEASPOONS BAKING POWDER
½ TEASPOON BAKING SODA
¼ TEASPOON BLACK PEPPER

4 TABLESPOONS COLD BUTTER, CUT
  INTO PIECES
1 CUP GRATED CHEDDAR CHEESE
¾ CUP MILK

1. Preheat the oven to 425°.

2. In a small skillet, cook the bacon over medium heat until crisp, about 10 minutes. Drain the bacon on paper towels; set aside.

3. In a medium bowl, stir together the flour, baking powder, baking soda, and pepper. With a pastry blender or 2 knives, cut in the butter until the mixture is coarse crumbs. Crumble in the bacon, then add the cheese and milk, and stir briefly to form a dough.

4. Transfer the dough to a lightly floured surface and knead for 1 to 2 minutes, adding up to 2 tablespoons more flour if necessary. Roll the dough out to a rectangle roughly 9 x 7 inches. With a floured knife, cut the rectangle into twelve 2¼-inch squares.

5. Place the biscuits on a baking sheet and bake for 12 to 15 minutes, or until golden. Serve hot.

DESSERTS

Oatmeal Raisin Cookies

MAKES 2 DOZEN

🕐 EXTRA - QUICK

1 CUP FLOUR

½ TEASPOON BAKING POWDER

½ TEASPOON SALT

1 STICK BUTTER, AT ROOM
   TEMPERATURE

¾ CUP DARK BROWN SUGAR

¼ CUP GRANULATED SUGAR

1 EGG

1 TEASPOON VANILLA EXTRACT

1 TABLESPOON MILK

1 ¼ CUPS ROLLED OATS

½ CUP RAISINS

1. Preheat the oven to 350°. Lightly grease 2 large baking sheets.

2. In a small bowl, combine the flour, baking powder, and salt; set aside.

3. In a large bowl, cream the butter, brown sugar, and granulated sugar until light and fluffy. Stir in the egg, vanilla, and milk, continuing to stir until the mixture is smooth.

Stir in the flour mixture, a little at a time, then add the oatmeal and raisins, stirring until well blended.

4. Drop the batter by tablespoonfuls onto the baking sheets, leaving enough space between them for the cookies to expand. Bake for 12 minutes, or until the cookies are lightly browned on top.

Variation: *Instead of the traditional raisins, use chopped pitted prunes, dried apricots, or dried figs; the fruit should be tender and moist (plump it briefly in boiling water if it's very dry and hard).*

Double Chocolate Chip Cookies

MAKES 2 DOZEN

🕐 EXTRA-QUICK

1 STICK BUTTER, AT ROOM
   TEMPERATURE
⅓ CUP GRANULATED SUGAR
⅓ CUP BROWN SUGAR
½ TEASPOON SALT
½ TEASPOON VANILLA EXTRACT
¼ TEASPOON COLD WATER

1 EGG
½ TEASPOON BAKING SODA
1 CUP FLOUR
4 OUNCES SEMISWEET CHOCOLATE
   CHIPS
4 OUNCES WHITE CHOCOLATE CHIPS

1. Preheat the oven to 375°. Lightly grease 2 large baking sheets.

2. In a large mixing bowl, combine the butter, sugars, salt, vanilla, and water, and beat them together with a large spoon until the mixture is light and fluffy. Beat in the egg and baking soda and when they are well combined add the flour, beating it in ¼ cup at a time. Gently but thoroughly fold in the semisweet chocolate and white chocolate chips.

3. Drop the cookie batter onto the baking sheets a tablespoonful at a time, leaving about 1½ inches between the cookies. Gently pat down the top of each cookie, but don't flatten entirely. Bake for about 12 minutes, or until the cookies are firm to the touch and lightly browned. Let the cookies cool on the baking sheets for about 1 minute, then transfer them to racks to cool.

Chunky Peanut Butter Cookies

MAKES 2 DOZEN

EXTRA-QUICK

1 CUP ROLLED OATS

1½ CUPS FLOUR

½ TEASPOON BAKING SODA

¼ TEASPOON BAKING POWDER

¼ TEASPOON SALT

1 STICK BUTTER, AT ROOM
 TEMPERATURE

½ CUP GRANULATED SUGAR

½ CUP BROWN SUGAR

1 EGG

½ CUP CHUNKY PEANUT BUTTER

½ TEASPOON VANILLA EXTRACT

1. Preheat the oven to 350°.

2. In a food processor or blender, process the oats until they are a fine powder; transfer to a medium bowl. Add the flour, baking soda, baking powder, and salt, and stir to combine.

3. In a large bowl, cream the butter, granulated sugar, and brown sugar until light and fluffy. Beat in the egg, peanut butter, and vanilla until well blended. Add the flour mixture and stir until well combined.

4. Shape rounded teaspoonfuls of dough into balls and place them on a baking sheet. Flatten each cookie in a crisscross pattern with a fork dipped in water.

5. Bake the cookies for 8 to 10 minutes, or until the edges just begin to brown. Let the cookies cool on the baking sheet for 1 minute, or until set, then transfer to racks to cool.

Variation: *When the cookies are cool, sandwich them in pairs, using strawberry jam as the filling.*

Butterscotch Fudge Brownies

1 CUP FLOUR

1½ TEASPOONS BAKING POWDER

⅔ CUP PLUS 3 TABLESPOONS BUTTER

2 CUPS LIGHT BROWN SUGAR

4 WHOLE EGGS PLUS 1 EGG YOLK

2½ TEASPOONS VANILLA EXTRACT

1½ CUPS CHOPPED WALNUTS

3 OUNCES SEMISWEET CHOCOLATE,
  BROKEN INTO PIECES

2 TABLESPOONS HEAVY CREAM

1. Preheat the oven to 350°. Line a 9-inch square baking pan with foil and lightly grease the foil.

2. In a small bowl, stir together the flour and baking powder; set aside.

3. In a small saucepan, melt ⅔ cup of the butter over medium-low heat. Add the sugar and stir constantly until the sugar dissolves, 10 to 12 minutes. Pour the mixture into a large bowl and let cool until tepid.

4. Beat the whole eggs, 1 at a time, into the cooled butter mixture, beating well after each addition. Beat in 2 teaspoons of the vanilla. Beat in the flour mixture, then fold in the walnuts. Spread the batter evenly into the prepared baking pan.

5. In a small saucepan, over low heat, melt the chocolate with the remaining 3 tablespoons butter. Beat in the cream and the remaining ½ teaspoon vanilla, then remove the pan from the heat and whisk in the remaining egg yolk.

6. Drizzle the chocolate mixture over the batter in the pan. Pull a knife through the batter to marbleize the butterscotch and chocolate batters. Bake for 1 hour and 15 minutes, or until a toothpick inserted into the center comes out clean.

7. Let the brownies cool in the pan on a rack before cutting into 9 squares.

TOASTED ALMOND BROWNIES

MAKES 20

½ CUP CHOPPED ALMONDS

4 OUNCES SEMISWEET CHOCOLATE

4 OUNCES UNSWEETENED CHOCOLATE

1 CUP FLOUR

1 TEASPOON BAKING POWDER

¼ TEASPOON SALT

2 STICKS BUTTER, AT ROOM
   TEMPERATURE

1⅔ CUPS SUGAR

3 EGGS

1 TEASPOON VANILLA EXTRACT

1. Preheat the oven to 350°. Grease and flour an 11 x 7-inch baking pan.

2. Toast the almonds in a small skillet over medium-high heat, shaking the pan frequently, until golden brown, 5 to 10 minutes; set aside to cool slightly.

3. Meanwhile, cut the semisweet chocolate and unsweetened chocolate into large pieces. In the top of a double boiler over hot, not simmering, water, melt the chocolate, stirring until smooth. Set aside to cool slightly.

4. In a small bowl, stir together the flour, baking powder, and salt; set aside.

5. In a large bowl, cream the butter and sugar until light and fluffy. Beat in the eggs, 1 at a time, beating well after each addition. Beat in the vanilla. Add the melted chocolate and mix until well blended, then gradually add the flour mixture, beating well after each addition. Stir in the almonds.

6. Spread the batter evenly in the prepared baking pan. Rap the pan on the counter to remove any air pockets. Bake for 45 to 50 minutes, or until the brownies shrink from the sides of the pan, and a toothpick inserted into the center comes out clean.

7. Let the brownies cool in the pan on a rack, then cut into 20 bars.

Apricot-Currant Biscotti

MAKES 48

3 CUPS FLOUR
1 TEASPOON BAKING POWDER
PINCH OF SALT
5 TABLESPOONS BUTTER
⅔ CUP SUGAR
3 EGGS

1 TABLESPOON GRATED LEMON ZEST
1 TABLESPOON FRESH LEMON JUICE
¾ TEASPOON ALMOND EXTRACT
1 CUP CURRANTS
¾ CUP CHOPPED DRIED APRICOTS

1. Preheat the oven to 350°.

2. In a medium bowl, combine the flour, baking powder, and salt; set aside.

3. In another medium bowl, cream the butter and sugar until light and fluffy. Beat in the eggs, 1 at a time, beating well after each addition. Beat in the lemon zest, lemon juice, and almond extract. Gradually add the flour mixture, beating constantly, until incorporated. Add the currants and apricots and beat until just combined.

4. Divide and shape the dough into two 2½-inch-thick loaves. Place them on a nonstick baking sheet and bake 30 minutes, or until just beginning to brown. Transfer the loaves to a rack and let them cool for 45 minutes.

5. Preheat the broiler.

6. Place the loaves on a cutting board and, with a serrated knife, cut them diagonally into ¾-inch-thick slices. Lay the slices on a baking sheet and broil 1 minute, or until lightly browned. Carefully turn the biscotti and brown another minute. Transfer them to a rack to cool.

Red, White, and Blue Pie

SERVES 8 TO 10

1½ CUPS FLOUR

2 TABLESPOONS PLUS ¼ CUP SUGAR

7 TABLESPOONS BUTTER, AT ROOM
   TEMPERATURE

4 TO 5 TABLESPOONS ICE WATER

5 CUPS STRAWBERRIES

2½ CUPS BLUEBERRIES

¼ CUP FRESH LEMON JUICE

3 TABLESPOONS COLD WATER

1 TABLESPOON CORNSTARCH

2 CUPS SWEETENED WHIPPED CREAM

1. In a large bowl, combine the flour and 2 tablespoons of sugar. With a pastry blender or 2 knives, cut in the butter until the mixture is coarse crumbs. Sprinkle 2 tablespoons of the ice water over the mixture and toss it with a fork. The dough should be just barely moistened, enough so it will hold together when it is formed into a ball. If necessary, add up to 3 tablespoons more water, 1 tablespoon at a time.

2. Preheat the oven to 400°.

3. On a lightly floured surface, roll the dough out to a 12-inch circle. Fit the dough into a 9-inch glass pie plate. Trim the overhang to an even ½ inch all the way around. Fold the overhang under and crimp the dough to form a decorative border. Prick the pastry with a fork.

4. Line the pie shell with foil, fill it with pie weights or dried beans, and bake for 10 min-

utes. Remove the foil and weights, reduce the oven temperature to 375°, and bake for another 10 to 12 minutes, or until light golden.

5. Place 1 cup of the strawberries and ½ cup of the blueberries in a small saucepan and crush them with a fork. In a small bowl, stir together the lemon juice, water, and cornstarch until blended, then add this mixture to the crushed berries. Stir in the remaining sugar, and cook over medium heat, stirring constantly, for 5 minutes, or until the mixture thickens and becomes translucent.

6. Place the remaining 4 cups strawberries and 2 cups blueberries in a medium bowl, pour the cooled berry glaze over them, and toss gently to coat. Spoon the berry mixture into the pie shell and refrigerate until serving time.

7. Just before serving, spoon or pipe the whipped cream decoratively on top of the pie.

Lemon-Orange Meringue Pie

ONE 9-INCH UNBAKED PIE CRUST,
STOREBOUGHT OR HOMEMADE
¾ CUP PLUS ⅓ CUP SUGAR
¼ CUP CORNSTARCH
3 TABLESPOONS FLOUR
1¾ CUPS MILK
4 EGGS, SEPARATED

⅓ CUP FRESH LEMON JUICE
2 TABLESPOONS BUTTER, CUT INTO
PIECES
1 TABLESPOON GRATED LEMON ZEST
1 TABLESPOON GRATED ORANGE ZEST
1 TEASPOON ORANGE EXTRACT
¼ TEASPOON CREAM OF TARTAR

1. Preheat the oven to 400°. Line the pie shell with foil, fill it with pie weights or dried beans, and bake for 10 minutes. Reduce the oven temperature to 350°.

2. In a medium saucepan, combine ¾ cup of the sugar, the cornstarch, and flour. Place the pan over medium heat and slowly add the milk, whisking constantly. Continue cooking and whisking until the mixture is thick enough to coat the back of a spoon. Remove the pan from the heat and let the mixture cool slightly.

3. Add the egg yolks, 1 at a time. Then add the lemon juice, and whisk until well blended. One ingredient at a time, add the butter, lemon and orange zests, and orange extract, whisking well after each addition; the custard should be very thick. Set the pan in a large bowl of cold water to cool for about 5 minutes.

4. Meanwhile, in a large bowl, beat the egg whites until frothy. Add the cream of tartar and continue beating until soft peaks form. Gradually add the remaining ⅓ cup sugar and continue beating until stiff, glossy peaks form.

5. Turn the cooled filling into the pie shell, spreading it evenly with a rubber spatula. Spoon the meringue on top, mounding it into peaks and being careful to have it meet the crust at the edges. Bake for 8 to 10 minutes, or until the meringue is lightly browned. Serve the pie slightly warm, or at room temperature.

Clown Birthday Cake

SERVES 8 TO 10

3 CUPS CAKE FLOUR
2 TEASPOONS BAKING POWDER
¼ TEASPOON SALT
2 STICKS BUTTER, AT ROOM
    TEMPERATURE
1½ CUPS SUGAR

3 EGGS
1 CUP BUTTERMILK OR PLAIN YOGURT
1 TEASPOON VANILLA EXTRACT
DECORATOR'S FROSTING
GUMDROPS, RED COLORED SUGAR,
    JELLYBEANS, CANDY SPRINKLES

1. Preheat the oven to 375°. Grease the bottoms of two 8-inch round cake pans, then line them with circles of wax paper. Grease and flour the wax paper.

2. In a medium bowl, combine the flour, baking powder, and salt; set aside.

3. In a large bowl, cream the butter and sugar until light and fluffy. Beat in the eggs, 1 at a time, beating well after each addition. Beat in the buttermilk and vanilla. Gradually add the flour mixture and beat until well blended.

4. Spread the batter evenly in the prepared pans. Rap the pans on the counter to remove any air pockets. Bake for 30 to 35 minutes, or until the cakes shrink from the sides of the pans and a toothpick inserted into the center of each cake comes out clean. Let the cakes cool in the pans for 10 minutes, then turn them out onto racks to cool completely before frosting.

5. Remove the wax paper from the cake layers. Cover a baking sheet or a large piece of cardboard with foil. Place 1 of the cake layers on the baking sheet for the clown's head. Cut off 3 sides of the other cake layer to form a triangle. Place the triangle above the clown's head for a hat. Cut a circle out of one of the remaining pieces of cake for the top of the hat, then cut the rest into cubes and arrange them at the bottom of the clown's head to form ruffles.

6. Set aside ½ cup of the frosting for decoration, then spread a generous layer of frosting over the top and sides of all the cake pieces. Refrigerate for 15 minutes to set the frosting.

7. Tint the remaining frosting black and use it to pipe the outlines for the eyes, nose and mouth. Use gumdrops for the pupils of the eyes. Fill in the nose and mouth with red colored sugar. Decorate the hat and ruffles with jellybeans and candy sprinkles.

Marbled Angel Food Cake

5 TABLESPOONS PLUS ½ CUP FLOUR
3 TABLESPOONS COCOA POWDER
1¼ CUPS SUGAR
⅛ TEASPOON SALT
10 EGG WHITES

1 TEASPOON CREAM OF TARTAR
1 TEASPOON ALMOND EXTRACT
½ TEASPOON VANILLA EXTRACT
1 TABLESPOON POWDERED SUGAR

1. Sift 5 tablespoons of the flour, the cocoa powder, and 2 tablespoons of the sugar into a medium bowl. Sift the cocoa mixture 3 more times and set the bowl aside.

2. Sift the remaining ½ cup of flour, the salt, and 2 tablespoons of remaining sugar into another medium bowl. Sift this mixture 3 more times and set it aside too.

3. Preheat the oven to 350°. Rinse out a tube pan and shake, but do not wipe it dry.

4. In a large bowl, beat the egg whites until soft peaks form. Add the cream of tartar, then blend in the remaining cup of sugar, a little at a time, beating until stiff peaks form. With the mixer set on the lowest speed, blend in the almond extract, then the vanilla. Transfer half of the beaten egg whites to a clean bowl.

5. Fold the dry cocoa mixture into one of the bowls of beaten egg whites. Pour the chocolate batter into the tube pan. Fold the remaining dry mixture into the beaten egg whites in the other bowl, and spoon the batter over the chocolate batter in the tube pan. Plunge a spatula down through both layers of batter, then bring it back to the surface with a twisting motion. Repeat this step at 1-inch intervals around the cake to marble the batter thoroughly.

6. Bake the cake for 45 minutes. Invert the pan (if your pan does not have "legs," slip the tube of the pan over the neck of a bottle) and let the cake cool completely. Run a knife around the sides of the pan to loosen the cake before turning it out. Sift the powdered sugar over the cake before serving.

Carrot Cake with Cream Cheese Frosting

SERVES 8 TO 10

2 CUPS FLOUR

3 TEASPOONS BAKING POWDER

¼ TEASPOON SALT

1 TEASPOON CINNAMON

½ TEASPOON NUTMEG

½ CUP VEGETABLE OIL

½ CUP GRANULATED SUGAR

¾ CUP BROWN SUGAR

2 EGGS

1 TEASPOON ALMOND EXTRACT

1 TEASPOON GRATED ORANGE ZEST

¾ CUP BUTTERMILK

2 CUPS GRATED CARROTS

½ CUP RAISINS

½ CUP CHOPPED WALNUTS

1 STICK BUTTER, AT ROOM
 TEMPERATURE

1 TABLESPOON MILK

1 TEASPOON VANILLA EXTRACT

1 POUND POWDERED SUGAR

8 OUNCES CREAM CHEESE, AT ROOM
 TEMPERATURE

1. Preheat the oven to 350°. Grease and flour two 8-inch round cake pans.

2. In a medium bowl, combine the flour, baking powder, salt, cinnamon, and nutmeg.

3. In a large bowl, beat the vegetable oil, granulated sugar, and brown sugar until creamy. Add the eggs, 1 at a time, beating well after each addition. Beat in the almond extract and orange zest. Alternating between the 2, beat in the flour mixture and the buttermilk, beating well after each addition. Stir in the carrots, raisins, and walnuts.

4. Pour the batter into the prepared cake pans. Bake for 30 to 35 minutes, or until a

toothpick inserted into the center of each cake comes out clean and the cake shrinks away from the sides of the pans. Cool the cakes in the pan on racks. Allow the cakes to cool completely before frosting.

5. Meanwhile, in a large bowl, beat the butter, milk, vanilla, and powdered sugar until smooth. Add the cream cheese and beat until the frosting is thick enough to spread.

6. Invert one of the cake layers onto a serving plate. Spread a generous layer of frosting on top of the cake layer. Place the second cake layer on top and frost the top and sides of the entire cake.

Almond Cheesecake
with Chocolate Crust

SERVES 8

15 GRAHAM CRACKER SQUARES

4 TABLESPOONS BUTTER

1 OUNCE SEMISWEET CHOCOLATE, CUT
INTO PIECES

½ CUP CHOPPED TOASTED ALMONDS

2 CUPS RICOTTA CHEESE

ONE 8-OUNCE PACKAGE CREAM
CHEESE, AT ROOM TEMPERATURE

ONE 8-OUNCE PACKAGE ALMOND PASTE

¼ CUP SUGAR

3 EGGS

1 TEASPOON VANILLA EXTRACT

1. Preheat the oven to 350°.

2. In a food processor or blender, process the graham crackers to fine crumbs; transfer the crumbs to a bowl and set aside.

3. In a small saucepan over low heat, melt the butter and chocolate, stirring until smooth. Add the chocolate mixture and the almonds to the crumbs, and stir to combine, then pat the crumb mixture into the bottom and halfway up the sides of an 8½ x 2½-inch round springform pan; set aside.

4. In a medium bowl, combine the ricotta, cream cheese, and almond paste, and beat until smooth. Beat in the sugar. Add the eggs, 1 at a time, beating well after each addition. Add the vanilla and beat until smooth.

5. Pour the filling into the crust. Bake for 1 hour, or until the filling is golden around the edges and begins to crack in the center. Let the cake cool completely in the pan on a rack.

6. To serve, place the pan on a serving platter, run a knife around the edge of the pan and remove the rim.

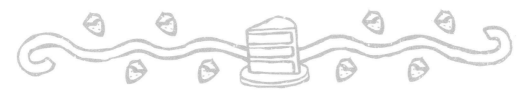

Pineapple Upside-Down Cake

SERVES 10

♡ LOW-FAT

2 TABLESPOONS PLUS ½ CUP BROWN
    SUGAR
ONE 20-OUNCE CAN JUICE-PACKED
    PINEAPPLE SLICES, DRAINED, 1 CUP
    OF JUICE RESERVED
⅓ CUP COARSELY CHOPPED DRIED
    APRICOTS

1½ CUPS FLOUR
1¼ TEASPOONS BAKING POWDER
½ TEASPOON BAKING SODA
PINCH OF SALT
¼ CUP BUTTER
1 EGG
1 CUP DARK RAISINS

1. Preheat the oven to 350°. Grease an 8-inch cake pan and sprinkle 2 tablespoons of the sugar in the bottom. Arrange the pineapple slices in the pan, overlapping them slightly, and fill the hole in each slice with apricots.

2. In a small bowl, stir together the flour, baking powder, baking soda, and salt; set aside.

3. In a medium bowl, cream the butter and the remaining sugar. Beat in the egg, then beat in the flour mixture and the reserved pineapple juice alternately, in 3 parts each.

Stir in the raisins. Pour the batter into the pan and rap it on the counter to remove any air pockets. Bake for 1 hour, or until the cake is golden and pulls away from the sides of the pan.

4. Let the cake cool on a rack for 5 minutes. Run a knife around the edge of the pan to loosen the cake, then place a serving plate over the pan and invert it. Tap gently, then carefully lift the pan to turn out the cake. Serve the cake warm or at room temperature.

New Mexican Chocolate Cake

SERVES 8 TO 10

2 CUPS FLOUR

¼ CUP COCOA POWDER

2 TEASPOONS CINNAMON

3 STICKS BUTTER, CUT INTO PIECES
PLUS 4 TABLESPOONS BUTTER, AT
ROOM TEMPERATURE

8 OUNCES SEMISWEET CHOCOLATE

1 CUP MILK

1 TEASPOON INSTANT ESPRESSO
POWDER

4 EGGS, SEPARATED

1½ CUPS SUGAR

1 TEASPOON VANILLA EXTRACT

½ TEASPOON SALT

⅓ CUP HEAVY CREAM

3 CUPS POWDERED SUGAR

1½ TEASPOONS INSTANT ESPRESSO
POWDER DISSOLVED IN 2 TEASPOONS
HOT WATER

1. Preheat the oven to 350°. Grease a 15 x 10 x 2-inch cake pan, line the bottom with greased wax paper, and flour the wax paper.

2. In a medium bowl, stir together the flour, cocoa powder, and cinnamon; set aside.

3. In a small saucepan, combine the pieces of butter, the chocolate, milk, and dry espresso powder. Cook over low heat, stirring until smooth. Set aside to cool slightly.

4. In a large bowl, beat the egg yolks and sugar until pale and lemon-colored. Add the cooled chocolate mixture and the vanilla, and beat until blended.

5. In another large bowl, beat the egg whites and salt until stiff peaks form.

6. Gradually add the flour mixture to the large bowl, beating well after each addition. Fold in the beaten egg whites.

7. Spread the batter evenly in the prepared pan. Rap the pan on the counter to remove any air pockets. Bake for about 30 minutes, or until a toothpick inserted into the center of the cake comes out clean.

8. Cool the cake in the pan for 10 minutes, then carefully turn it out onto a rack to cool completely.

9. Meanwhile, in a medium bowl, beat together the cream and remaining butter until smooth. Gradually add the powdered sugar, beating until smooth and fluffy. Add the espresso mixture, and beat until blended. Spread the icing over the top and sides of the cake.

BERRY-ORANGE ICE CREAM CAKE

SERVES 8 TO 10

1⅓ CUPS CAKE FLOUR
¾ TEASPOON BAKING POWDER
¼ TEASPOON SALT
5 EGGS, SEPARATED
1¼ CUPS SUGAR
3 TABLESPOONS MILK

2 TEASPOONS GRATED ORANGE ZEST
¼ TEASPOON ORANGE EXTRACT
½ TEASPOON CREAM OF TARTAR
1 PINT STRAWBERRY ICE CREAM,
    SOFTENED
2 CUPS SWEETENED WHIPPED CREAM

1. Preheat the oven to 350°. Line the bottom of a 13 x 9-inch baking pan with wax paper. Grease and flour the pan.

2. In a small bowl, stir together the flour, baking powder, and salt.

3. In a large bowl, beat the egg yolks and sugar until the mixture is pale and lemon-colored. Beat in the milk, orange zest and extract. Gradually beat in the flour mixture, beating well after each addition.

4. In another large bowl, beat the egg whites until frothy. Add the cream of tartar and continue beating until stiff peaks form. Gently fold the egg whites into the batter.

5. Spread the batter evenly in the prepared pan. Bake for 25 to 30 minutes, or until the cake shrinks from the sides of the pan and a toothpick inserted into the center of the cake comes out clean. Let the cake cool in the pan

for 10 minutes, then turn it out onto a rack to cool completely before assembling.

6. Remove the wax paper from the cake. Cut the cake in half lengthwise to form 2 layers. Place one layer of cake on a large sheet of foil.

7. Spread the ice cream over the bottom layer, then cover it with the second layer, pressing it down lightly. Wrap the cake in the foil and place it in the freezer until the ice cream is firm, at least 3 hours, or overnight.

8. Just before serving, trim the sides of the cake with a long, serrated knife to create a smooth surface. Transfer the cake to a serving platter.

9. Reserve ¾ cup of whipped cream for decorating, then spread a thick layer of whipped cream over the top and sides of the cake. Pipe the reserved whipped cream decoratively around the edges of the cake.

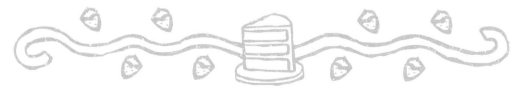

STRAWBERRY SHORTCAKE

2 CUPS FLOUR
½ TEASPOON SALT
2 TEASPOONS BAKING POWDER
½ TEASPOON BAKING SODA
½ TEASPOON CREAM OF TARTAR
2 TABLESPOONS PLUS ¼ CUP SUGAR
1 STICK BUTTER, AT ROOM TEMPERTURE

⅔ CUP BUTTERMILK
1 PINT FRESH STRAWBERRIES, SLICED
OR ONE 16-OUNCE PACKAGE FROZEN
SLICED STRAWBERRIES, THAWED
SWEETENED WHIPPED CREAM

1. Preheat the oven to 350°. Grease a large baking sheet.

2. In a large bowl, combine the flour, salt, baking powder, baking soda, cream of tartar, and 2 tablespoons of sugar. With a pastry blender or 2 knives, cut the butter into the flour mixture until it is coarse crumbs. Add the buttermilk all at once and stir until the dough forms a ball.

3. Transfer the dough to a floured surface and with floured hands knead 10 times. Pat the dough out to ½ inch thick. With a floured 3-inch biscuit cutter, cut out 8 circles Reroll and cut out any scraps of dough. Place the circles on the prepared baking sheet. Bake for 10 to 12 minutes, or until the edges begin to brown. Transfer the shortcakes to racks to cool slightly.

4. Meanwhile, in a medium bowl, combine the strawberries and the remaining sugar; set aside.

5. Cut the warm shortcakes in half, spoon some strawberries and a dollop of whipped cream on top.

RASPBERRY SOUFFLÉ

SERVES 6

♡ LOW-FAT

2 TABLESPOONS PLUS ½ CUP SUGAR
2 CUPS FRESH OR FROZEN RASPBERRIES, THAWED

2 EGG WHITES
⅓ CUP POWDERED SUGAR

1. Lightly grease a soufflé baking dish. Sprinkle 2 tablespoons of the sugar evenly in the dish, then tilt and rotate the dish to coat it thoroughly with the sugar. Refrigerate the dish until ready to use.

2. In a food processor or blender, purée the raspberries. Strain the purée through a fine sieve and set aside.

3. Preheat the oven to 400°. Pour the egg whites into a large bowl. Have the electric mixer ready.

4. In a small saucepan, combine the remaining ½ cup of sugar with ¼ cup of water. Bring the mixture to a boil over medium-high heat and continue boiling until the water has nearly evaporated and the sugar itself begins to cook.

5. Begin beating the egg whites on high speed. Pour the sugar mixture down the side of the bowl in a very thin, steady stream. When all the sugar has been incorporated, decrease the speed to medium and continue beating until stiff peaks form and the mixture has cooled to room temperature, 5 to 10 minutes. Increase the speed to high and beat for 1 minute.

6. Stir about one-third of the egg white mixture into the raspberry purée, then fold in the remaining meringue. Pour the mixture into the prepared baking dish, slightly overfilling it. Level the top with a spatula, then run the tip of your thumb around the inside of the dish; the resulting circular depression will keep the edges of the soufflé from burning as the dessert puffs up in the oven. Sift a little of the powdered sugar over the top. Bake the soufflé until it has risen and is set, about 25 to 30 minutes. Serve immediately.

Quick Chocolate Mousse

SERVES 8 TO 10

EXTRA-QUICK

3 CUPS HEAVY CREAM
6 OUNCES MINI SEMISWEET
   CHOCOLATE CHIPS
1 TABLESPOON CHOCOLATE LIQUEUR

1 TEASPOON VANILLA EXTRACT
¼ CUP POWDERED SUGAR
CHOCOLATE SHAVINGS, FOR GARNISH

1. In a small saucepan, warm ½ cup of the cream over low heat until almost simmering. Remove the pan from the heat and stir in the chocolate chips. Cover and set aside for 5 minutes, then stir until the chocolate chips are melted and the mixture is smooth. Transfer the mixture to a large bowl and stir in the liqueur and vanilla.

2. In another large bowl, beat 1½ cups of cream with the sugar until soft peaks form.

Fold ½ cup of the whipped cream into the chocolate mixture, then gently fold in the remaining whipped cream. Chill the mousse until ready to serve.

3. In a large bowl, beat the remaining cup of cream until stiff peaks form.

4. Serve the chocolate mousse in parfait glasses, topped with whipped cream and chocolate shavings.

KITCHEN NOTE: *Crème de cacao is a chocolate-flavored liqueur that comes in "white" (clear) and brown versions; either will do for this recipe. You could substitute a coffee liqueur for a change.*

CHOCOLATE FONDUE

SERVES 8 TO 10

⏲ EXTRA-QUICK

12 OUNCES SEMISWEET CHOCOLATE,
    CUT INTO PIECES
½ CUP HEAVY CREAM
2 CUPS CUBED ANGEL FOOD CAKE OR
    LADYFINGERS
1 APPLE, CUT INTO WEDGES

1 ORANGE, PEELED AND SEPARATED
    INTO SECTIONS
1 PINT FRESH WHOLE STRAWBERRIES,
    STEMS LEFT ON
1 CUP PINEAPPLE CHUNKS
2 BANANAS, CUT INTO 2-INCH SLICES

1. In a fondue pot or flameproof casserole dish, combine the chocolate and cream and cook over very low heat, stirring constantly, until the chocolate is melted and the mixture is smooth.

2. Keep the fondue warm over a very low flame. Arrange the angel food cake, apple, orange, strawberries, pineapple, and bananas on a platter, accompanied by spears for dipping.

VARIATION: *Chocolate fondue may be flavored with kirsch (a clear cherry liqueur) or with orange liqueur, such as Grand Marnier. Stir 3 tablespoons of liqueur into the fondue just before serving.*

BEVERAGES

·ORANGE LEMONADE

MAKES 32 CUPS

EXTRA-QUICK ♡ LOW-FAT

6 QUARTS ORANGE JUICE
6 CUPS FRESH LEMON JUICE

6 ORANGES, SLICED
6 LEMONS, SLICED

1. Pour the orange and lemon juices into a large bowl and stir well.

2. Refrigerate the orange lemonade until well chilled, then add the sliced oranges and lemons. Pour some of the beverage into a large pitcher and refill as needed.

MELON COOLER

SERVES 8

EXTRA-QUICK ♡ LOW-FAT

8 POUNDS WATERMELON
5 POUNDS CANTALOUPE

SMALL MELON WEDGES AND FRESH
MINT LEAVES, FOR GARNISH

1. Remove the watermelon flesh from the rind. Seed the flesh and cut it into large cubes. Quarter the cantaloupe and cut off the rind. Cut the cantaloupe flesh into large chunks.

2. Place the watermelon and cantaloupe in a food processor or blender and process until puréed. Strain the purée into a pitcher, cover, and refrigerate until well chilled. At serving time, stir well and garnish each glass with a skewer of melon wedges and mint leaves.

Tangerine-Raspberry Juice

SERVES 6

⏰ EXTRA-QUICK ♡ LOW-FAT

TWO 10-OUNCE PACKAGES FROZEN RASPBERRIES, THAWED

16 TANGERINES

1. Place the raspberries and their juice in a food processor or blender and process until puréed. Force the mashed berries through a fine sieve set over a bowl to remove the seeds. Transfer the sieved purée to a pitcher.

2. Halve and squeeze the tangerines; strain the juice into the pitcher and stir well. Cover and refrigerate until serving time.

3. Stir the juice mixture to blend it before serving.

Sparkling Fruit Punch

SERVES 6 TO 8

⏰ EXTRA-QUICK ♡ LOW-FAT

3 CUPS UNSWEETENED APPLE JUICE
2½ CUPS UNSWEETENED WHITE GRAPE JUICE
1 CUP UNSWEETENED CRANBERRY JUICE
1 CUP FRESH LIME JUICE

1 QUART GINGER ALE OR SPARKLING WATER
LEMON OR LIME SLICES, FOR GARNISH (OPTIONAL)

1. In a large pitcher or punch bowl, stir together the apple, grape, cranberry, and lime juices. Add the ginger ale and stir briefly.

2. Garnish the punch with lemon or lime slices, if desired.

Sunny Sangria

MAKES 4 QUARTS

♡ LOW-FAT

4 LEMONS

4 LIMES

3 ORANGES

1 PINK GRAPEFRUIT

1 QUART PINEAPPLE JUICE

24 OUNCES WHITE GRAPE JUICE

1 RED APPLE, THINLY SLICED

1 CUP STRAWBERRIES, LIGHTLY
   CRUSHED PLUS WHOLE
   STRAWBERRIES FOR GARNISH

1. Wash and thinly slice 1 lemon, 1 lime, and 1 orange, and place the slices in a punch bowl. Halve and squeeze the grapefruit and the remaining lemons, limes, and oranges, and pour the juices into the punch bowl. Add the pineapple and grape juices to the bowl, then add the apple slices and crushed strawberries, and stir well. Cover the bowl and refrigerate the sangria for at least 2 hours.

2. Just before serving, stir the sangria again and add the whole strawberries.

Rum Punch

SERVES 8

🕐 EXTRA-QUICK   ♡ LOW-FAT

4 OUNCES FRESH LIME JUICE

4 TABLESPOONS SUPERFINE SUGAR

12 OUNCES LIGHT OR DARK RUM

16 OUNCES WATER

15 ICE CUBES

8 THIN ORANGE SLICES

1. Combine the lime juice, sugar, rum, water and ice cubes in a pitcher and stir with a wooden spoon.

2. Pour the punch through a strainer into a punch bowl, garnish with orange slices, and serve at once.

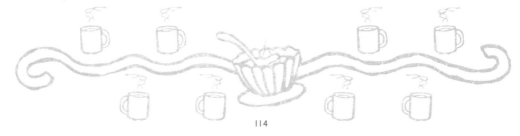

CHAMPAGNE PUNCH

MAKES 2 QUARTS

1 ORANGE, PEELED AND SEPARATED
INTO SECTIONS
6 MARASCHINO CHERRIES
1 CUP FRESH LEMON JUICE
1 CUP BRANDY

½ CUP MARASCHINO LIQUEUR
½ CUP CURAÇAO
1 QUART CHAMPAGNE, CHILLED
1 PINT CLUB SODA, CHILLED

1. Place the oranges in a large punch bowl. Stir in the cherries, lemon juice, brandy, maraschino liqueur, and curaçao. Refrigerate the bowl for at least 1 hour.

2. Just before serving, pour the champagne and club soda into the punch bowl. Stir briefly and serve.

Mimosa

SERVES 8

🕐 EXTRA-QUICK ♡ LOW-FAT

16 OUNCES FRESH ORANGE JUICE
24 OUNCES CHAMPAGNE

8 WHOLE STRAWBERRIES, FOR GARNISH
(OPTIONAL)

1. In a large pitcher, combine the orange juice and champagne.

2. If using, cut a slit in the bottom of each strawberry. Slide a strawberry onto the edge of a stemmed glass.

3. Fill each glass with the mimosa mixture and serve.

Banana Daiquiri

SERVES 8

🕐 EXTRA-QUICK ♡ LOW-FAT

2 MEDIUM BANANAS, COARSELY
   CHOPPED
16 OUNCES LIGHT RUM
2 OUNCES BANANA LIQUEUR

2 OUNCES FRESH LIME JUICE
2 CUPS CRUSHED ICE
SUPERFINE SUGAR

1. In a blender, combine the banana, rum, liqueur, lime juice, and ice. Blend at high speed for 20 to 30 seconds, until the banana is completely pulverized and the mixture is smooth and frothy.

2. Taste the mixture and add superfine sugar if necessary. Pour the daiquiri mixture into 8 glasses and serve immediately.

Ice Cream Sodas

SERVES 8

🕐 EXTRA-QUICK

48 OUNCES ROOT BEER
8 SCOOPS CHOCOLATE ICE CREAM
WHIPPED CREAM

CHOCOLATE SHAVINGS
8 MARASCHINO CHERRIES

1. Pour 6 ounces of root beer into each of 8 tall glasses. Carefully drop a scoop of ice cream into each glass.

2. Pipe a whipped cream rosette onto each ice cream soda, sprinkle with chocolate shavings, and top with a maraschino cherry.

Mocha Milk Shakes

2 TABLESPOONS BUTTER
2 OUNCES UNSWEETENED CHOCOLATE, CUT INTO PIECES
1 CUP SUGAR

PINCH OF SALT
1½ TEASPOONS VANILLA EXTRACT
1 CUP MILK
3 CUPS COFFEE ICE CREAM

1. In a medium saucepan, melt the butter with the chocolate over very low heat, stirring constantly until the mixture is smooth.

2. Remove the pan from the heat and stir in the sugar, salt, and ½ cup of water. Return the pan to the stove and cook over medium heat, stirring frequently, for 5 minutes. Stir in the vanilla. Cool the chocolate sauce to room temperature before using.

3. In blender combine the milk, chocolate sauce, and ice cream and blend until thick and frothy. Serve immediately.

Mint Cocoa

8 CUPS MILK
¾ CUP COCOA POWDER
½ CUP CRÈME DE MENTHE

1 CUP SUGAR
MINIATURE MARSHMALLOWS, FOR GARNISH

1. In a medium saucepan, stir the milk, cocoa powder, crème de menthe, and sugar over low heat until hot.

2. Pour the cocoa into mugs and garnish with marshmallows.

Irish Coffee

SERVES 6

⏰ EXTRA-QUICK

6 TEASPOONS SUGAR

6 OUNCES IRISH WHISKEY

36 OUNCES STRONG, HOT COFFEE

½ CUP WHIPPED CREAM

1. Spoon a teaspoon of sugar into each of 6 glass mugs or stemmed goblets. Pour 1 ounce of whiskey and 6 ounces of coffee into each mug. Stir to dissolve the sugar.

2. Top each Irish coffee with a dollop of whipped cream.

Hot Spiced Cider

MAKES 16 CUPS

♡ LOW-FAT

10 WHOLE CLOVES

3 SMALL CINNAMON STICKS, PLUS ADDITIONAL STICKS FOR GARNISH (OPTIONAL)

1 GALLON APPLE CIDER

2 LEMONS, SLICED, PLUS ADDITIONAL SLICES FOR GARNISH (OPTIONAL)

1. Place the cloves and cinnamon sticks in a double thickness of cheesecloth, fold it into a packet, and fasten it with string.

2. Pour the cider into a large pot, add the spice packet and the 2 sliced lemons, and bring to a simmer. Simmer the cider for 30 minutes; do not let it boil.

3. Ladle the cider into mugs. Garnish with additional cinnamon sticks and lemon slices, if desired.

Spring Breakfast Buffet

Tangerine-Raspberry Juice
(PAGE 113)

Blueberry Crepes
(PAGE 78)

Banana Pancakes with
Strawberry Sauce (PAGE 72)

Zucchini and Cheese Quiche
(PAGE 81)

Glazed Peach Coffeecake
(PAGE 83)

Birthday Party

Ice Cream Sodas
(PAGE 116)

Vegetable Pizza
(PAGE 33)

Clown Birthday Cake
(PAGE 100)

Open House

Rum Punch (page 114)

Vermont Cheddar Spread
(page 13)

Mini Crab Cakes
(page 12)

Spinach and Cheese Squares
(page 25)

Apricot-Currant Biscotti
(page 97)

Candlelight Dinner

Spinach Salad
(page 68)

Wild Rice with Mushrooms
and Pecans (page 61)

Roast Leg of Lamb with
Mint Sauce (page 51)

Raspberry Soufflé
(page 108)

Irish Coffee (page 118)

Fiesta Buffet

Sunny Sangria (PAGE 114)

Fresh Salsa with Toasted
Tortillas (PAGE 22)

Zesty Guacamole
(PAGE 23)

Chicken Fajitas with
Red Peppers (PAGE 50)

Beef Tacos (PAGE 49)

New Mexican Chocolate Cake
(PAGE 105)

Picnic in the Park

Orange Lemonade (PAGE 112)

Oven-Baked Potato Chips
(PAGE 15)

Three-Bean Salad (PAGE 65)

Seafood Salad Sandwiches
(PAGE 41)

Herbed Oven-Fried Chicken
(PAGE 30)

Double Chocolate Chip Cookies
(PAGE 93)

Summer Barbecue

Melon Cooler
(PAGE 112)

Potato Salad with
Bacon Bits (PAGE 66)

Barbecued Spareribs with
Orange Sauce (PAGE 31)

Red, White, and Blue Pie
(PAGE 98)

Afternoon Baby Shower

Sparkling Fruit Punch
(PAGE 113)

Date-Nut Bread (PAGE 88)

Lemon-Orange Meringue Pie
(PAGE 99)

Marbled Angel Food Cake
(PAGE 101)

Carrot Cake with
Cream Cheese Frosting (PAGE 102)

COCKTAIL PARTY

Banana Daiquiri
(PAGE 116)

Rum Punch (PAGE 114)

Vegetarian Pâté (PAGE 28)

Stuffed Mushroom Caps
(PAGE 8)

Hummus with Toasted
Pita Wedges (PAGE 20)

Cheese Fondue (PAGE 26)

HEARTY SUNDAY BRUNCH

Mimosa (PAGE 115)

Bacon-Cheddar Biscuits
(PAGE 90)

Blueberry Buttermilk Pancakes
(PAGE 73)

Huevos Rancheros
(PAGE 82)

Mini Apple-Walnut
Coffeecakes (PAGE 84)

Super Bowl Snacks

Spicy Buffalo
Chicken Wings (page 10)

Potato Skins with
Sour Cream and Chives (page 11)

Pork Wontons (page 19)

Vegetable Pizza (page 33)

Toasted Almond Brownies
(page 96)

Chunky Peanut Butter Cookies
(page 94)

Holiday Feast

Scandinavian-Style Canapés
(page 27)

Caesar Salad (page 69)

Scalloped Potatoes (page 55)

Stuffed Roast Turkey
(page 52)

Almond Cheesecake with
Chocolate Crust (page 103)

Hot Spiced Cider (page 118)

Index